LONDON

AUTHENTIC RECIPES CELEBRATING THE FOODS OF THE WORLD

Recipes and Text
SYBIL KAPOOR

Photographs
JEAN-BLAISE HALL

General Editor
CHUCK WILLIAMS

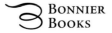
BONNIER
BOOKS

UNDERGRO
A DAY ON ATKINS
www.atkins.com/uk
Earls Court
Putney High Street
South Kensington
WVL24
VOLVO
First

CONTENTS

RECIPES

42 A. GOLD. French Milliner 42

RICHARD
WOODALL's
FINEST
CUMBRIAN
BACON

THE FINEST
SAUSAGES
FROM
CUMBRIA

IAN THOMAS *Licensed to Sell Beers, Wines, & Spirits OFF the Premises*

OPEN

A. GOLD ~ Traditional Foods of Britain

LOCALLY
BREWED
ORGANIC
ALE

INTRODUCTION

Two thousand years ago, the Romans built an outpost on the river Thames where London's financial district now stands. The population of the settlement was surprisingly international. This character still pervades every aspect of the metropolis, especially its cuisine, a sophisticated fusion of British creativity and global influences.

CULINARY HISTORY

The blueprint of London cooking was first laid down by the Romans. Around AD50 they founded a settlement called Londinium at a ford on the river Thames. At this hub, the Romans began to build a network of roads that soon gave them access to most of Britain and established a port that eventually grew into a centre for global trade. The troops occupying the settlement's fortifications came from what is now Syria, Spain, and Italy, as well as other areas within the vast Roman empire. As a result, the population of Londinium was extraordinarily international.

These new residents learned where to harvest native game and fish, and where to obtain local livestock, fruits, and vegetables. The dishes they prepared were Anglo-Roman in style – classic Roman fare such as stuffed roast rabbit was made using local English ingredients. The upper class seasoned their food with imported delicacies such as olive oil, raisins, wine, pine nuts, and liquamen, a fermented fish sauce.

Little is known of London's culinary tastes after the Roman legions departed in AD410.

There is no doubt, however, that the arrival of William the Conqueror from France in 1066 changed the city's cooking for ever. The new king of England insisted on replacing Anglo-Saxon customs and cuisine – rooted in local produce, roast game, and stewed red meat with herb sauces – with French customs and Norman preferences in food. The roast and sautéed meat and fowl of Norman cuisine were heavily spiced and were served with complicated aromatic sauces containing such ingredients as almonds, ginger, and sugar.

Growing prosperity

By the thirteenth century, London had developed into a bustling, rich commercial city and a centre of political and royal power. This growth in prosperity and sophistication was manifested in the range of dishes prepared by cooks and served primarily at the tables of nobility: distinctly English roasts, grilled meats, and savoury pies, as well as newly adopted French sautés, fricassées, and sauces. Various roasted, fried, and boiled foods were the specialities of cookshops, early

eating establishments open all hours of the day. Londoners had an immense appetite for meat, fowl, and seafood, from Welsh lamb and Scottish beef to oysters from the Thames. Their love of onions, garlic, and leeks was so great that onions had to be imported from Holland and garlic from France and Spain.

Imported delicacies

Because London was a centre of international trade, the city's inhabitants welcomed the arrival of new foods. If nobles desired a meal of pigeons stewed with pepper, ginger, and saffron, or royal cooks wanted to introduce Italian dishes like macaroni with butter and Parmesan, merchants would import the necessary ingredients. Knowledge of these new recipes and ingredients was spread across the capital by the city's cooks, who belonged to a guild, the Cooks' Company, established in the 1300s.

As competition for the spice trade intensified, Britain sought to import ever larger quantities of spices and seasonings, including sugar. In the sixteenth century, London bakers

began to turn out wonderful spiced and fruited buns such as gingerbread and hot cross buns, and cooks added a variety of spices such as cloves, cinnamon, and fennel to savoury meat pies, mince pies, and sweet fruit tarts made with pears or apples. Even the ale houses, early ancestors of the pub (see page 50), spiced their brews by warming ale with ginger, nutmeg, cloves, sugar, and the pulp of tart crab apples to make a drink called lamb's wool. A notable English beverage owes its origins to Britain's robust trade: tea from China was introduced to London in the 1640s by the East India Company, formed to import spices and other goods from the Far East (see page 36).

A culinary style takes shape

As Britain thrived over the next few centuries, Londoners enjoyed ever better food. The quality of the livestock, seafood, dairy products, and fresh fruits and vegetables brought into the city's vast markets was superb compared to what was sold in many other European cities. This plentiful and high-quality supply meant that foods did not have to be overcooked or heavily seasoned to mask their lack of taste or freshness. Instead, the city's cooks created simple dishes that celebrated the particular character of a few well-chosen ingredients. Rather than make a complicated, time-consuming French stew with tough and often stringy mutton shanks, cooks could now purchase and roast a tender leg of lamb, then accompany it with home-made redcurrant jelly. A syllabub of cream with wine and sugar was as delicious as, and took less time to make than, a traditional steamed pudding. Such straightforward dishes, using good-quality ingredients, were regarded as typically English.

This style of cooking reached its zenith during the eighteenth century. At the same time, Londoners continued to dine on an international selection of dishes, just as they had in earlier centuries. Books such as Hannah Glasse's *The Art of Cookery Made Plain and Easy* (1747) and Elizabeth Raffald's *The Experienced English Housewife* (1769) included recipes for Indian curry, Turkish mutton, and Portuguese beef. London cooks could buy all the ingredients they needed to make these recipes – spices, dried fruits, chillies, tamarind, olive oils, and vinegars – from specialist food shops.

Global influences

One factor that contributed to this broad and varied palette was the arrival of immigrants from around the world, who came to seek their fortune or flee from difficult circumstances in their native countries. The Italians had a particularly marked impact on the London diet. Not only did they open shops that sold imported foods, but they also established confectionery shops that made and sold sweets such as ices and gelatos. The most famous was Gunter's Tea Shop in Berkeley Square, founded by Domenico Negri in 1757 and named for his British partner, James Gunter, who later operated the shop on his own. At inexpensive Italian restaurants in

Soho and Clerkenwell, avant garde Londoners dined on roast chicken, imported olives, and brandied cherries while sipping Marsala.

Culinary consolidation

The nineteenth century, when London rapidly expanded into a vast metropolis, was a period of culinary consolidation. The Anglo-French style of cooking, combining both French and English recipes, remained the foundation of London cookery. It still dominated the city's tables and was served in many of the grand restaurants and banquet halls. Some of these survive, such as Simpson's Grand Restauratum in the Strand – today called Simpson's-in-the-Strand – founded in 1848, and the Café Royal on Regent Street, dating from 1865. Working Londoners dined on roast meats, crusty breads, and locally brewed beer in neighbourhood restaurants known as ordinaries, or sipped wine while enjoying savoury meat and fish pies, hearty stews, and grilled meats at local taverns, the forerunners of wine bars. Street vendors sold steaming bowls of pea soup, creamy baked potatoes, fried fish, and other simple dishes that made up an inexpensive meal.

Yet the dramatic social and economic changes in the twentieth century, brought about in part by two world wars, inevitably impacted London's eating habits. A decreased interest in home cooking and a reliance on processed food led to the city's reputation for bland, overcooked fare. It would take many years before Londoners would slowly begin to rediscover fine home cooking.

A new direction

It was primarily through the evocative writings of Elizabeth David and Robert Carrier that Londoners were reintroduced to home cooking and seasonal cuisine. David extolled the pleasures and rewards of preparing Mediterranean dishes such as Provençal ratatouille and Italian minestrone, and the importance of using proper ingredients like the highest quality extra virgin olive oil and the freshest basil. Robert Carrier, an American by birth, introduced Londoners to the concept of glamorous, well-made dishes that drew on influences from around the world, whether a fine French pâté or a Greek moussaka. From these roots, French nouvelle cuisine in particular became popular for its fresh, light approach to cooking.

In the 1960s and 1970s, Londoners began to travel more widely than before on holidays, not only to Spain, Italy, Greece, and other European countries but to other continents. Back at home, they could satisfy their enthusiastic appetite for ethnic foods by eating at the Chinese, Indian, Turkish, and Thai restaurants that were opening up in many neighbourhoods throughout London. Unfamiliar ingredients such as Indian garam masala, Chinese lotus roots, and Thai kaffir lime leaves began to appear in specialist shops and delicatessens (see page 42), allowing cooks to prepare ethnic dishes at home. Although many Londoners still had their favourite Anglo-French classics, many others were discovering something new.

CONTEMPORARY CUISINE

London has undergone a remarkable culinary renaissance that emphasises seasonal foods and ethnic flavours. Sparked by pioneering chefs, the trend has been embraced by home cooks, who eagerly seek out locally grown produce at farmers' markets and artisanal products in the city's many specialist food shops.

Most Londoners would have difficulty defining London cuisine, even though many enjoy cooking at home in their leisure time and food is a favourite topic of conversation. Nevertheless, if you were to peek into their kitchens throughout the year, you could gain a sense of the typical London diet.

Seasonal cuisine

In winter, the preference is for warming dishes such as puréed vegetable soups, fragrant Moroccan tagines with preserved lemons, rich Kashmiri curries, Chinese stir-fries, tender roast leg of lamb with redcurrant jelly, roast partridge with a classic bread sauce, and buttery fruit pies. Summer is the season for lighter fare: for example, Lebanese-style grilled chicken with herbed yoghurt sauce, Mediterranean pastas and salads, barbecued fish and meat, fruit salads, and home-made ice cream. Indian and Chinese takeaways are universally popular, and most Londoners admit to a great fondness for pungent flavours such as soy sauce, chillies, lime leaves, fresh coriander, and lemongrass.

Simply prepared English dishes made with ingredients in season are integral to London's cuisine. In spring it might be an asparagus vinaigrette made with the highly regarded English crop (see page 109) followed by grilled lamb cutlets; in summer, it is poached salmon with fresh mayonnaise and then strawberries and cream. Not only do these foods taste delicious, they make Londoners feel a strong connection with the surrounding countryside by reminding them of the changing seasons. Enjoying a steak and wild mushroom pie, roast pheasant, or pan-fried venison steak followed by an apple and blackberry pie or a pear syllabub in a London restaurant in October or November reinforces the arrival of autumn and conjures up images of long country walks and cosy rural pubs.

The arrival of farmers' markets

The link between town and country has been strengthened in recent years by the increasing number of farmers' markets that have opened across the city. Currently there are at least a dozen farmers' markets scattered throughout London, from Blackheath in the East to Swiss Cottage in the North and Wimbledon in the South. The first farmers' market was opened in Islington in June 1999. All of these markets are dependent on local government and community support to ensure that the market space is reserved and set up on a weekly basis.

Farmers drive in to the London markets from up to 160 kilometres (100 miles) away, and many specialise in unusual produce such as tatsoi (an oriental green), wild garlic, golden beetroots, and elderberries. Locally made buffalo cheese, smoked trout, and wild game such as mallard and partridge can also be found at many of the markets. Many of these foods are difficult if not impossible to

find in supermarkets or smaller food shops, and Londoners take pleasure in being able to talk directly to farmers. Farmers, in turn, will give their customers helpful suggestions for preparing unfamiliar foods, and will even forage for certain hard-to-find wild foods, such as elderflowers or wild plums, if their customers make a special request. Farmers' markets have become so popular in London that more and more open every year.

Reviving artisanal food

Coinciding with the popularity of farmers' markets is the revival of small artisanal food shops. Many of these disappeared in the 1970s and 1980s with the proliferation of supermarkets. The quality of the merchandise sold at these shops and the skills of the proprietors were sorely missed by food-loving Londoners, who now relish visiting a butcher who orders goose, pork, or beef directly from their favourite farms throughout Britain. They can also visit a cheesemonger who encourages them to sample Stilton from

Nottinghamshire, Wigmore from Berkshire, or a selection of local farmhouse Cheddars.

Restaurant pioneers

The renewed interest in artisanal foods was pioneered by London's chefs, who, frustrated with the limited range of fruit and vegetables, meat, seafood, and other items available from restaurant suppliers, began to do their own sourcing of ingredients. Smiths of Smithfield, for example, a lively, informal restaurant adjoining the Smithfield meat market, sought out rare breeds of pigs, sheep, and beef such as Gloucester Old Spot and Tamworth pigs, and Welsh Black beef.

Fergus Henderson, co-owner and head chef of the internationally recognized restaurant St John, looked for the highest quality ingredients for his "nose to tail" cooking. Many of his renowned specialities are classics that he has revived and updated, such as melt-in-the-mouth roast bone marrow and parsley salad served with sea salt and country bread, succulent braised oxtail,

and tender suckling kid with fennel compote. Restaurants across the ethnic spectrum follow the same approach. Assaggi, a relaxed, stylish Sardinian restaurant in Chepstow Place, W2, for example, imports the finest Sardinian specialities, including wafer-thin *carta da musica* (music-paper bread) and *bottarga* (grey mullet roe).

Since Londoners are familiar with cuisines from around the world, it is a natural step for them to experiment at home by adapting the foods and flavours from other cultures into their recipes. What makes these dishes unique to London is that they adhere to the concept of combining a few well-balanced ingredients. Thus, asparagus might be grilled Italian style and dressed in a Japanese-influenced sesame and soy dressing, or a leg of lamb might be marinated Middle Eastern style with lemon juice, olive oil, yogurt, cumin, and onion before it is roasted. In either case, the aim remains the same – to create a dish where the best features of each of the components are enhanced.

EATING OUT

Enjoying a meal at a dining mecca owned by a trend-setting chef or at a local gastropub or ethnic restaurant is the essence of social life in London. Residents have more than ten thousand choices, and the city can compete with Paris in its number of Michelin-starred restaurants.

London has an extraordinarily diverse population. A 2003 survey found that the city's schoolchildren speak about three hundred different languages. With people of various nationalities living side by side throughout the city, many neighbourhoods have a wide range of ethnic restaurants. Chinese, Indian, and Italian places are as common today in London as its many pubs and wine bars. In most areas, people have the choice of these and other ethnic restaurants, including Lebanese, Greek, Thai, Japanese, and French. In some neighbourhoods, traditional British restaurants such as fish and chip shops are becoming harder and harder to find.

Global cuisine

Ethnic restaurants are among Londoners' favourites, and they usually base their selection on both food and atmosphere. Woodlands in Marylebone Lane, for example, is perfect for a quick, inexpensive vegetarian Indian meal after a day of shopping. Casually dressed diners never feel out of place while sipping mango lassi (a yoghurt drink) and eating crisp *dosa* (a South Indian pancake) with vegetable curry and coconut chutney. At the Real Greek in Hoxton Market, N1, groups of friends like to feast on oven-baked giant butter beans and grilled smoked sausages encased in warm rye bread, finishing with Metaxa brandy and sultana ice cream. The

superlative Chinese food at the Michelin-starred Hakkasan in Hanway Place, W1, with its glamorous ambience and opulent, dimly lit interior, is often the choice for a special occasion. After savouring enoki mushroom and prawn dumplings and roast silver cod with Champagne and Chinese honey, diners are ready to visit a nightclub or bar and party until the early hours of the morning.

Simple masterpieces

Londoners are equally drawn to the myriad restaurants and gastropubs whose cooking may variously be described as Italian, modern British, Mediterranean, or Spanish. Their chefs share an interest in simply prepared, seasonal dishes that highlight the flavour of the core ingredients. A well-known exponent of this approach is the River Café in Rainville Road, W6, where diners can sit outdoors beside the Thames and order black truffle risotto, pasta parcels filled with ricotta cheese and wild greens, or baked wild sea bass with treviso. Fino in Charlotte Street, W1, with its interior of red leather and blond wood, serves delectable Spanish tapas such as sautéed clams in sherry and tiger prawns with aioli. Robust Spanish and North African cuisine – grilled aubergine and red pepper salad with flatbread, wood-roasted sardines served with preserved lemons, coriander, and warm potato salad, and yoghurt and pistachio cake for dessert – is the speciality at the critically

acclaimed minimalist restaurant Moro, located in Exmouth Market, EC1.

For formal occasions, Londoners are spoiled by the sheer number of Michelin-starred restaurants scattered across the capital. The majority serve a contemporary London version of Anglo-French or Italian food. Among the best are Gordon Ramsay in Royal Hospital Road, SW3, and Locanda Locatelli in Seymour Street, W1. Gordon Ramsay's restaurant, with its cool purple interior and quiet staff, has a very discreet air, and every dish reflects his restrained, elegant approach. Texture and flavour are perfectly balanced, from the turbot poached in red wine to the celeriac risotto to the baked chocolate fondant with orange sorbet. Giorgio Locatelli, the chef behind Locanda Locatelli, epitomizes the current London interpretation of Italian cooking in his light-filled, retro-style restaurant. Using superlative ingredients, he makes such simple, creative Italian dishes as seared scallops with saffron puréed potatoes or an almond fondant pudding with pistachios.

Pub life

Socialising with colleagues is a common ritual in London, and towards the end of the week, groups of workers head for a nearby pub or wine bar for lunch or an after-work drink. It is hard to walk from one street to the next in London without finding a bar or pub, and part of the enjoyment is discovering a new establishment hidden in a mews or tucked down a narrow passage. The small, wood-panelled Jerusalem Tavern in Britton Street, EC1, converted from a house built in 1720, is particularly popular in winter, when the regulars gather round the fire in the small front parlour and sip the chocolatey winter ale made by St Peter's Brewery in Suffolk. The Barley Mow in Dorset Street, W1, dating from 1791, is frequented mainly by local workers, who sit outside on the wooden benches in good weather and drink Green King IPA or Marston's Pedigree beer. Many pubs offer simple, traditional dishes, such as bangers and mash with onion gravy or a ploughman's lunch of crusty bread, a wedge of crumbly

cheese, and fruity pickle. Others serve roast chicken, hearty steak pies with mash, and on Sundays, a traditional lunch of roast beef, lamb, or pork, with all the trimmings.

Neighbourhood restaurants

For most Londoners, the neighbourhood where they live is an extension of their home. Meeting up with friends at a local gastropub or an ethnic restaurant is a far more informal and relaxed occasion than going further afield. So regularly do Londoners visit their local pizzeria or Chinese or Indian restaurant that they often know the menus by heart.

Relishing the variety available close to their doorstep, Londoners enjoy ordering a superb takeaway – Vietnamese *banh xeo* (chicken and bean sprout pancakes), Turkish grilled kebabs, Chinese squid with black bean sauce, or Indian chicken tikka masala or prawn curry – as much as they love cooking in their own kitchens. Once at home, they can open a bottle of fine wine and await the arrival of friends to enjoy their meal together.

MARKETS

Bustling markets with their winter greens and rosy apples are as much a part of London's heritage as its fine houses and lush parks. Today's farmers' markets, like the older street markets, are a source of good food and lively discourse. They are also re-establishing the ancient link between town and country.

Every day vast quantities of food are brought into London by road, rail, ship, and airplane to feed the population of nearly 7.4 million residents. Most of the food is sold through supermarkets, but a significant quantity goes to wholesale markets: Covent Garden (fruits and vegetables as well as flowers), Great Western (fresh produce from Asia), Smithfield (a wide range of meat), and Billingsgate (fish and shellfish). Each market has independent wholesalers who source food from around the world to supply London's hotels, restaurants, and street markets.

Londoners can visit these markets and buy their produce direct, provided they are prepared to get up very early. Since most of the city's chefs have fallen into bed around the time the markets start their daily business, they prefer to rely on specialist restaurant suppliers instead. By 3AM each weekday morning, the wholesale markets are humming with activity. Friendly banter fills the chilly dawn air as fresh produce is examined, haggled over, and sold, then reloaded onto vans and lorries and taken to London's street markets or small shops. Some wholesale markets stay open longer to complete the restaurant orders left by chefs at the end of their night shift. Vans carrying the orders are soon on the road, delivering wild mushrooms or crayfish to restaurants needing them before 9AM.

London's wholesale markets are extraordinary places. Only Smithfield remains in the City on its original 1174 site. Its elegant building, dating to 1868, was modelled on the glass-and-iron Crystal Palace of 1851 and has been thoroughly modernised. Billingsgate, founded in 1016, moved from its Roman dock on the Thames to Docklands in 1982. The romantic seventeenth-century Covent Garden was rehoused in modern facilities at Nine Elms, Battersea, in 1973.

Strolling into the vast halls of modern Billingsgate at around 4AM, you will see a staggering array of gleaming fish. One wholesaler might specialise in wild Irish salmon, Scottish lobster, and Dover sole, while his neighbour concentrates on imported exotics such as tropical parrot fish, pomfret, and marlin. Sellers wearing white coats and Wellington boots pick their way purposefully across the wet floors before heading upstairs to complete their paperwork in the offices above the market. Meanwhile, the buyers, often fishmongers themselves, might grab a mug of sweet tea in the building's café before loading up their purchases and heading off to work.

As the wholesale markets wind down, the sellers at the street markets set up their stalls. Street markets have come and gone over the centuries, depending on London's needs. With the rise of supermarkets that buy direct from growers, street markets and independent small shops have declined. All of the market stalls are licensed by their local councils to trade at agreed times. Brixton

Pork, Chicken,
Apricots,
& Herb Stuffing

Half - £5.00
Pie - £10.00

Pork & Blue
Stilton Chees

£5.00

Market, for example, sells a glorious array of West Indian and African foods such as casavas, plantains, and callaloo, as well as pigeon peas, catfish, and goat meat. Ridley Road Market in the East End offers a mixture of English, West Indian, and Asian foods. Each market sells ingredients suited to the local population: for instance, Notting Hill's Anglo-Caribbean shops in Portobello Road sell pomelos and chillies; Edgware Road's Anglo-Asian Church Street Market displays Indian beans and white radishes called *mooli;* and Soho's continental Berwick Street offers traditional French and Italian foods such as frisée and white asparagus. Each costermonger, or street barrow-seller, bellows out prices and tries to lure customers in with lively banter and a fine display of his goods.

The introduction of farmers' markets and fine food markets has energized London's food scene. In 1999, with the opening of the first farmers' market in Islington, shoppers could meander around the stalls and talk to the people who actually made pork pies from

their own pigs in Somerset or grew their own gooseberries. Since Londoners enjoy dreaming about an idyllic rural life, this direct link to the countryside captured their imaginations. The success of this first market ensured that others would follow – Marylebone, Notting Hill, and Peckham. The markets also created a much-needed outlet for farmers who had been selling to supermarkets through wholesale markets.

London farmers' markets each have different traders, but the atmosphere is much the same, as crowds flock to a car park that has been transformed into a village fête. Tables spill over with fresh Malden oysters, crusty bread, pearly legs of Jacob lambs, Norbury blue cheese, lush bunches of baby turnips, and sprays of wild elderflowers. According to market rules, stall holders can only sell food that has been made, grown, or harvested within a 160-kilometre (100-mile) radius of London. Thus, English Preserves, a London-based business, uses local farm-grown fruit to make traditional preserves such as pear butter and quince cheese.

In 2000 a small wholesale market tucked under the railway arches at Borough, next to Southwark Cathedral, began holding a monthly specialist food market on Friday and Saturday mornings in an effort to regenerate the area. It rapidly became the haunt of food writers, who in turn made it a very popular destination for the public. Before long, Borough Market was open every week. Crowds thronged the market to soak up the atmosphere, enjoy roast chicken sandwiches, and buy wonderful specialist foods ranging from freshly roasted coffee to London honey. You can assemble a dinner party menu in minutes by pushing your way through the crowds to Turnips, where you can buy tomatoes, basil, peaches, and figs, or to Brindisa, where you can select saffron and rice for paella, or salt cod, olive oil, vinegars, and almonds. Chefs drop in to Borough Market to seek out new suppliers. Many of the stall holders, such as the Ginger Pig and L'Artisan du Chocolat, became so popular that they expanded into smart retail premises across London.

FLAVOURS OF THE NEIGHBOURHOODS

One of the best ways to explore London is to talk to the locals and quiz them about where and what they eat. Your search for food will lead you to discover the hidden side of London, from a cabbie's favourite fish-and-chip shop to a food lover's secret vice, a fabulous shop that specialises in cookery books.

Despite its vast size, London is made up of many small neighbourhoods. Each is a world within itself, housing countless different nationalities, cultures, and foods. Every district is filled with intriguing shops, restaurants, cafés, and bars. Some date back centuries; others are creating the latest trends.

The South Bank

A pedestrian walk that runs along the south side of the Thames, the South Bank links the Royal Festival Hall with the Hayward Gallery and Shakespeare's Globe Theatre. In recent years it has become a mecca for Londoners who like to brunch at Tate Modern and view the exhibits before strolling along to Borough Market to buy food for the weekend, such as coffee from Monmouth Coffee House, cheese from Neal's Yard Dairy, and cakes from Konditor & Cook. Many also walk eastwards to enjoy the view of the Tower of London while eating simple modern British dishes such as beetroot salad with horseradish and poached egg or roast pigeon with balsamic vinegar and sage at the Blueprint Café in the Design Museum. For some, there is nothing better than a play at the National Theatre or the Old Vic, followed by a takeaway of crisp-fried cod from Masters Super Fish in Waterloo Road.

The City and East End

At the heart of London lies the City, with its shimmering office blocks, medieval churches,

and Roman ruins. This is the capital's financial centre, yet its past endures in old markets such as Spitalfields, Leadenhall, and Smithfield. Tiny ancient pubs are tucked away down narrow passages. Among its superb restaurants are Smiths of Smithfield and Club Gascon. The former serves hearty dishes of rare-breed meats, such as grilled Longhorn rump steak, while the latter offers a constant flow of small plates, such as smoked zander (a white freshwater fish) on a hot stone. Heading up Commercial Street, you'll find the utilitarian-looking St John Bread & Wine, where the Whitechapel crowd of artists hangs out and enjoys simple British food, from a bacon sarnie to rhubarb ice cream. A few more steps eastwards and you will be in Brick Lane, with its colourful Bengali shops such as the Taj stores and a branch of the Ambala Sweet Centre.

Soho

During the day Soho has a slightly scruffy, Bohemian feel, beloved of its residents, whom you will often find sipping a cappuccino or an espresso in one of the many Italian bars, grabbing a spicy Caribbean bite at Mr Jerk, or wandering down Berwick Street Market to buy some asparagus or early Jersey Royals for supper. The area abounds with free-thinking media and celebrity types who hang out in private clubs such as the Groucho Club. Restaurants range from Soho institutions like

L'Escargot and Pollo, the latter offering inexpensive Italian fare, to relative newcomers, among them the elegant Lindsay House, serving superlative Irish food in pared-down eighteenth-century rooms. At night, Soho is transformed by the young pleasure-seekers who throng its many restaurants, bars, pubs, and clubs. Favourites are Yauatcha, Milk & Honey, and Ronnie Scott's Jazz Club.

Chinatown

Chinatown is renowned for its bustling chaos and rude manners, both of which Londoners enjoy, regarding them as integral to the area's unique atmosphere. The narrow streets are filled with Chinese restaurants, gambling clubs, supermarkets, and other businesses, as well as tourists. During the day, boxes of durian fruit, water spinach, and other exotic produce spill out from crowded shops like Loon Fung Supermarket and S W Trading Ltd. Dim sum addicts queue up at restaurants such as Chuen Cheng Ku, Royal Dragon, or New World, especially at weekends, to feast on yam rolls, lobster dumplings, and sautéed turnip paste. At night, the restaurants fill with diners eager to sample the steamed crab doused in Shaoxing wine at Mr Kong, the famous wind-dried meat dishes at Poons, and the Shanghai cuisine served at Ecapital.

Knightsbridge

The well-heeled shoppers who frequent Knightsbridge like to dress up before they go out. They live in the hushed world of embassies, five-star hotels, and the fashion stores that stretch from Hyde Park to Sloane Square. Rather than venture into a super-market, they prefer to order a cold lobster and *fraises de bois* from the food halls of Harvey Nichols or Harrods, and choose from a glittering array of Michelin-starred restau-rants including Nahm, serving classic Thai food; Zafferano, with its stylish, modern Italian menu; and Foliage, Pétrus, and the Capital Restaurant, which offer a distinctively London style of British-French cooking. With the exception of the discreet Zafferano, all are housed in hotels. The young set likes to hang out at Zuma, known for its elegant Japanese food, and at Mr Chow's, where superb Chinese food is presented in a glamorous setting.

Chelsea

This sprawling area that runs from Knights-bridge down to the Thames was once the haunt of artists and punk rockers. It is now dominated by wealthy thirty-somethings who spend their time buying wares in David Mellor's lovely kitchen shop. When shopping for food, they buy their groceries from the chic food shops of Elizabeth Street and pick up choco-lates from L'Artisan du Chocolat. Most impor-tant, some of London's finest restaurants are close by, including the eponomously named establishments of chefs Gordon Ramsay and Tom Aikens. London's best Indian restaurant, Rasoi Vineet Bhatia, is also in Chelsea.

Notting Hill

Notting Hillbillies, as they are known, are unlike other Londoners in their combination

of flashiness and social conscience. The area where they live stretches from Notting Hill to Ladbroke Grove and Westbourne Park Road. This was one of the city's first neighbourhoods to have organic shops such as Fresh & Wild and Planet Organic. Notting Hill is also home to Books for Cooks in Blenheim Crescent, laid-back gastropubs including the Cow and the Oak, and the stylish yet unpretentious Sardinian restaurant Assaggi, whose dining room is above a pub in Chepstow Villas. Those in search of local glitz tend to hang out at the pan-Asian fusion restaurant E&O, while those who prefer to be transported to a more unusual part of the world might go to Mandola, a tiny Sudanese restaurant.

Southall

Suburban Southall has been an Indian neighbourhood since the 1950s. Every weekend, its main street, the Broadway, is transformed into a bustling Indian bazaar filled with the scent of spicy grilled kebabs and the blare of Bhangra music. The crowd jostles and pushes good-naturedly as people stop to bargain for a box of guavas or eye up the queue for Indian sweets in the Ambala Sweet Centre. Traditionally dressed women stock up on spices, pulses, and pickles at shops like Sira Cash & Carry before gazing into the jewellery shops. Late into the night, entire families treat themselves to *chaat* at the brightly lit Gifto's Lahore Karahi or a meal at popular Madhu's, where Kenyan Punjabi food is served.

Marylebone

Marylebonites are a social breed who love the gentle pace of their eighteenth-century neighbourhood with its stylish shops and weekly farmers' market. The area stretches south from Marylebone Road to Oxford Street and west from Great Portland Street to Edgware Road. Pâtisserie Valerie on Marylebone High Street and the many pubs, such as the Marylebone Tup or Dusk, are popular with local residents. The area is filled with restaurants, ranging from the casual, yet elegant No 6 on George Street to the sophisticated Michelin-starred Orrery, which serves contemporary French food. Other favourites include fish and chips at the Golden Hind and exceptional Italian food at Locanda Locatelli.

Mayfair

The grand sweep of Park Lane separates Mayfair from the green open spaces of Hyde Park. Bordered on the south by Green Park, on the north by Oxford Street, and on the east by Regent Street, Mayfair is home to some of London's grandest hotels, including the Ritz, the Dorchester, Claridges, the Connaught, and the Metropolitan, as well as some of London's well-known Michelin-starred restaurants. The Gavroche serves classic French food, while the Square offers superb modern British food. Londoners love Mayfair's elegant streets, whether for brunch at Le Truc Vert after a walk in the park, lunch at Nicole's after window shopping in Bond Street, or a teatime treat at Sketch. The neighbourhood's tiny lanes contain hidden gems such as small pubs where locals can savour a pint of beer.

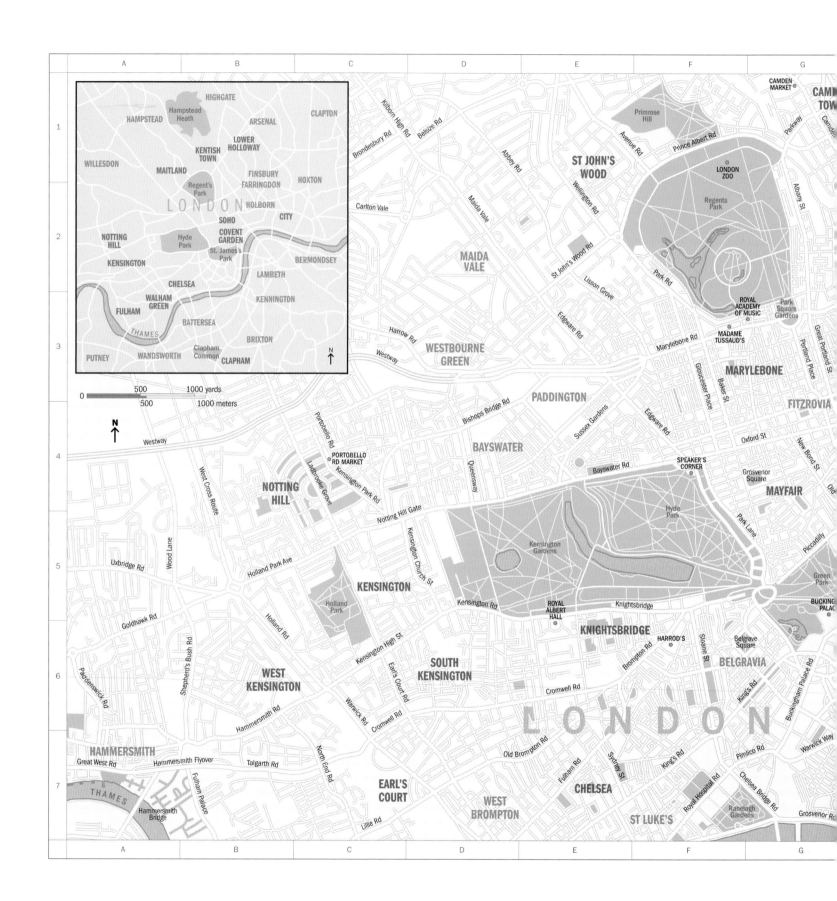

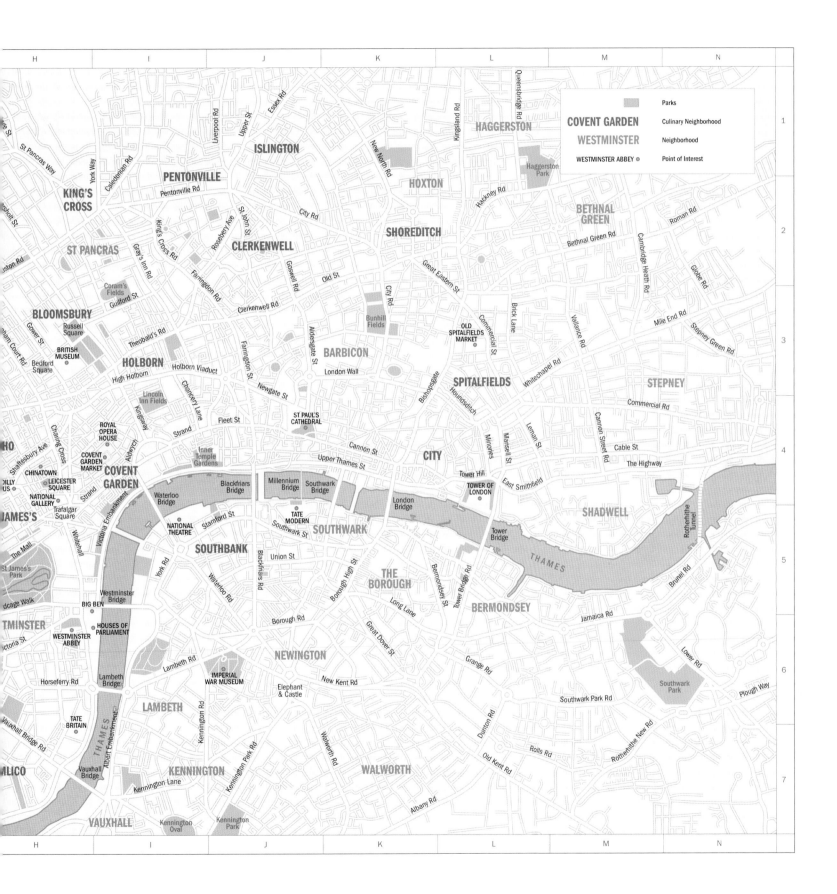

Best of **LONDON**

The thought of afternoon tea conjures rich images, from a lavish spread in the drawing room of a grand country house to the eccentricities of the Mad Hatter and his outsized teapot in *Alice's Adventures in Wonderland.* No matter where it is enjoyed, teatime is a treat – without it, life would be much less pleasurable.

AFTERNOON TEA

In gentler times, the ceremony of afternoon tea had a certain grace. Women would dress in their best frocks and would sport both hats and gloves. The event served more than the mere social function of meeting and gossiping, however. It was an occasion at which people could be entertained informally, without the rigidity that often pervaded lunch or dinner.

It was de rigueur to offer a tiered cake stand of dainty sandwiches – always including thinly sliced cucumber on buttered white bread – scones, jam-filled sponge cake, and fruit cake, alongside a plate of toasted and buttered crumpets or muffins. For a Devon cream tea, home-made jam and clotted cream were, and remain, the traditional accompaniments for the scone. Politeness dictated that you began with the savoury items before moving on to the sweet.

The art of laying a table for tea was almost as important as the food itself. There would be a white lace tablecloth, lace-edged linen napkins, fine bone china, a highly polished silver tea service, and, perhaps, a mother-of-pearl jam spoon with which to delve into the cut-glass jam pot. Teacups would be rinsed out with hot water before pouring in the tea, to prevent the delicate china from cracking.

Afternoon tea was particularly fashionable during the Edwardian period between 1901 and 1910. When the Argentinian tango arrived in Britain in 1910, London's grand hotels began to host tea dances, to the accompaniment of a live orchestra. By the early 1920s, the tea dance had become so popular that it continued to be an important social event until World War II. Many venues in London still maintain the tradition of the tea dance today, encouraged by the recent revival of interest in ballroom dancing.

In contrast to the high style of tea in grand hotels such as the Savoy, the Connaught, and the Ritz, many tea drinkers enjoy the bosky romance of The Orangery in Kensington Gardens. Others prefer the sleek sophistication of Sketch in Conduit Street, W1, whose tiny cakes can be savoured with an exquisite cup of jasmine tea. The wit of the "Prêt-à-Portea" served in the Caramel Room at the fashionable Berkeley Hotel draws a stylish clientele. Each tiny sandwich or miniature cake is inspired by the latest fashion on the season's catwalks. For a more exotic approach, Londoners visit Yauatcha in Broadwick Street, W1, which offers delectable cakes in the French tradition but with an oriental twist, and an extraordinary range of Chinese teas.

The quintessentially British ritual is an indulgent respite during a busy day.

VICTORIA
SPONGE

COCONUT RASPBERRY
SLICES

FINGER
SANDWICHES

HOT CROSS
BUNS

LEMON MERINGUE PIE

VICTORIA SPONGE

Named after Queen Victoria, who liked to serve it at teatime, this plain but delicious cake has the perfect balance of ingredients, achieved by matching the weight of the eggs in their shells with the same weight each of softened butter, sugar, and self-raising flour. The light sponge mixture is baked in two cake tins until golden. Once cooled, it is typically sandwiched with raspberry jam and whipped cream or buttercream, then dusted liberally with icing sugar.

LEMON MERINGUE PIE

Londoners are partial to all kinds of lemon tarts. Lemon meringue pie is a favourite for tea or as a dessert. A crisp shortcrust pastry case is filled with tangy lemon curd and topped with meringue. The original recipe is thought to date back to 1868.

COCONUT RASPBERRY SLICES

Biscuits are a daily essential, often eaten with a midmorning cup of coffee or as part of the afternoon tea offerings. Chewy variations, such as these shortbread slices with raspberry jam and coconut, are very popular.

FINGER SANDWICHES

Delicate and dainty, slender finger sandwiches, with their crusts cut off, are the epitome of an elegant afternoon tea. Three fillings are traditional. Two are served on white bread – wafer-thin slices of cucumber, and egg mayonnaise with cress – whereas brown bread is preferred for sandwiches of sliced smoked salmon seasoned with a squeeze of lemon juice and a fine grinding of pepper. Tea sandwiches should be prepared close to serving time to ensure freshness and then served on a plate lined with a paper or lace doily to absorb any moisture.

HOT CROSS BUNS

Made from a rich yeast dough that is deliciously spiced with nutmeg and cinnamon and fruited with currants or raisins, hot cross buns – split, toasted, and buttered – are traditionally eaten on Good Friday. Each bun is marked on top with a cross, either cut into the dough or made with pastry strips. Marking a cross on a bun or small cake is an ancient practise – at one time it was thought to ward off evil spirits that might prevent the buns from rising during baking. Today the cross marked on the bun is taken to represent Christ's crucifixion.

JOLLY RICH
FRUIT CAKE

COFFEE AND
WALNUT CAKE

SCONES

FONDANT FANCIES

CRUMPETS

COFFEE AND WALNUT CAKE

Every tearoom and cake shop in London offers a tempting array of cakes in all shapes and sizes. An enduring favourite is the coffee and walnut cake. Made from layers of moist walnut sponge sandwiched together by thick coffee buttercream, it is topped with the same rich buttercream or, occasionally, with coffee fondant icing. Walnut halves or chopped walnuts are used for decoration. Every customer expects to be served a large slice, blissfully closing their eyes as they savour their first bite.

FONDANT FANCIES

For afternoon tea, many of the grand London hotels present a silver tier filled with tiny cakes. No selection is complete without a few fondant fancies: squares of light sponge topped with buttercream and coated with fondant icing.

CRUMPETS

An established favourite, crumpets are made from a thick, yeasted batter that is cooked in crumpet rings on a lightly greased griddle. One side is smooth, while the other is perforated with tiny holes. Crumpets are served toasted with lashings of butter.

JOLLY RICH FRUIT CAKE

Londoners often take a slice of moist fruit cake on a long walk or to picnics in the park, because a rich fruit cake is like an energy bar – tightly packed with raisins, sultanas, and currants. It contains little sugar, flour, and eggs. The dried fruit is often macerated in rum or brandy before the other ingredients – candied peel, cloves, cinnamon, allspice, and nuts – are added. The baked cake can also be "fed" with a spirit or liqueur for an added kick. Northerners, in particular from Yorkshire and Lancashire, like to eat fruit cake with Cheddar cheese.

SCONES

Originating in Scotland, the scone is a staple of British afternoon tea. Made from a fairly plain dough, scones were traditionally cooked on a girdle (griddle), but nowadays are baked in the oven. They are best when served warm, split and liberally buttered. Sweet scones contain a little sugar and sometimes sultanas or currants, and are delicious with clotted cream and jam. The savoury variety can include such additions as Cheddar cheese or fresh herbs.

Londoners were formally introduced to the charms of tea in 1664, when the East India Company began to import it from China. Coffeehouses soon sold tea for home consumption – a habit that Catherine of Braganza, wife of Charles II, encouraged through her own predilection for the beverage.

TEA MERCHANTS AND TEA

By 1707, when Fortnum & Mason began to sell tea, it was well established as a fashionable, if expensive, drink. While men enjoyed it in coffeehouses, gentlewomen made clear green or black tea in the Chinese style, without milk or sugar, for their guests in the evening. Then, in 1717, Thomas Twining opened a tea shop – known by the sign of the Golden Lyon – in Devereux Court, WC2, and established the tradition of respectable ladies going out for tea. Tea gardens such as those at Ranelagh and Vauxhall followed, where all and sundry drank tea, danced, and watched public entertainments.

Tea only became widely available to the poor in 1784 when the government removed the high excise duty on tea leaves. Mid-morning tea breaks were routine by the end of the nineteenth century. At many firms, a

"tea lady" was employed to wheel a trolley around the office, which carried a vast urn of strong black tea, milk, sugar, and biscuits. The creation of afternoon tea, or simply 'tea' as it is known, is credited to Anna, seventh Duchess of Bedford, who, in the early 1800s, grew so hungry between lunch and dinner that she served tea with nibbles at four or five in the afternoon. "High tea" developed in the north of England during the nineteenth century, when working families merged tea and supper to create a single meal at 6PM, at which various cold meats, breads, and cakes were accompanied by tea.

Today, tea consumption has been revitalised with the availability of rare and unusual varieties from such companies as Twinings and Fortnum & Mason. Fortnum's, as it is affectionately known, has furnished

many a larder with a caddy of one of its famous teas, of which there are some 140, including the popular Royal Blend – a combination of Ceylon and Assam – dating from the coronation of Edward VII in 1902. Twinings and Fortnum's have been trading tea for nearly three hundred years. Twinings's museum, at the back of its shop, is well worth visiting, and its Lady Grey tea – a sumptuous blend of Chinese leaves and orange and lemon peel, flavoured with a hint of bergamot – is the perfect item to take home as a memento. Whittard, a relative newcomer since 1886, has done much to promote tea as a twenty-first century drink. It has many outlets, and those in fashionable Covent Garden and Carnaby Street have Tea Zones, stations where you can create customised blends by combining the leaf and flavour of your choice.

Confidences are often exchanged over a fragrant cup of tea.

Appreciated centuries ago for its reviving qualities, a cup of sweet, strong tea is still regarded by many Londoners as a cure-all for minor ailments and fatigue. It is as though the very act of putting on the kettle helps set the world right. Morning, noon, or night, the fragrance of brewing tea helps soothe the spirit and compose the mind.

The Bramah Museum of Tea and Coffee

Since tea is a national institution, it is not surprising that London is home to the world's first museum celebrating the drinking of it. The Bramah Museum of Tea and Coffee near London Bridge has a collection of historical tea-making ephemera and an adjoining tearoom. It sells everything you need for a perfect cuppa: a range of specialist teas, teapots, cosies, strainers, jugs for milk and hot water, sugar bowls, and tongs.

Understanding tea

Tea is made from the leaves of two different evergreen bushes. One is *Camellia sinensis,* which originated in China. The slightly larger-leafed, more prolific *Camellia assamica,* originated in Assam. There are three main categories, defined by how tea is processed: green (unfermented), black (fermented), and oolong (semi-fermented). For green tea, the leaves are dried immediately after picking to prevent oxidation and activation of the enzymes that change the taste of the tea. This ensures that the tea retains a fresh, almost grassy taste. In contrast, leaves for black tea are wilted to reduce moisture, bruised by rolling, and then allowed to brown further by contact with air so they oxidise. Oxidation gives black tea a full and complex taste. Oolong teas, made from large-leafed plants, are partially oxidised. The best are Formosa oolongs. White teas, predominantly from the downy tips of the unopened leaf bud, are dried naturally in the sun. Tea can also be classified by its country of origin and by the size of the tea leaves.

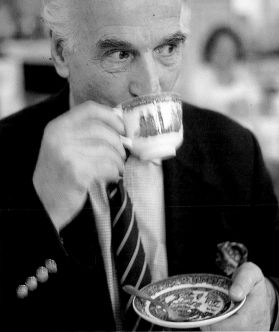

Making the perfect pot of tea

BOILING THE WATER The water should be brought just to the boil for brewing black tea and be just off the boil, at 70–88°C (160–190°F), for preparing more delicate green or white teas. The ideal pot for brewing tea contains a small, perforated holder for the tea leaves. The holder can be removed or sealed with a plunger once the tea has been brewed sufficiently.

BREWING THE TEA LEAVES The teapot is warmed with hot water just before the leaves are added. Traditionally, British tea drinkers allow 1 teaspoon of loose-leaf tea per person, plus 1 extra teaspoon for the pot, but most tea experts recommend experimenting to taste. Large-leaf teas can be brewed for 4–5 minutes; small-leaf teas need only 2–3 minutes.

SERVING THE TEA Tea may be drunk black or white (with milk), or with a slice of lemon. There is much debate about the correct way to serve the milk, but most believe that to prevent the milk from tasting scalded, it should be poured into the cup before the tea is slowly added.

BREAKFAST

CAMOMILE INFUSION

EARL GREY

JASMINE

BREAKFAST

If the British feel strongly about one culinary subject, it is their breakfast beverage. Tea drinkers are appalled at the idea of drinking coffee in the morning, while coffee drinkers cannot abide tea. Most tea drinkers love the strong, full-bodied taste of a traditional English breakfast tea, a blend of black Assam and Ceylon teas, which they drink with milk. Some prefer the even stronger Irish breakfast tea, a blend of Assam and Kenyan teas that is renowned for its robust taste. Both are perfect for enhancing the delights of bacon, eggs, and toast with marmalade.

CAMOMILE INFUSION

Londoners are very fond of herbal infusions, or tisanes, where a flower or herb is steeped in hot water to extract its flavour. They particularly like organic camomile, which is drunk late at night as a relaxant. Perforated sachets of the dried camomile flowers are infused with barely boiled water for about 3 minutes to release the delicate, fresh flavour.

EARL GREY

The flowery scent of bergamot wafting on the afternoon air is sufficient to alert everyone that it is tea time. The aroma comes from Earl Grey, a British tea created in the eighteenth century reputedly in honour of the second Earl Grey. Traditionally, it is made by flavouring a blend of black Darjeeling and China teas with oil of bergamot, an intensely aromatic variety of orange. Some brands of Earl Grey include a touch of Lapsang Souchong, which imbues the tea with a smoky taste. Earl Grey is perfect for afternoon tea, preferably without lemon or milk.

JASMINE

Long a London favourite, jasmine was first sipped in Chinese restaurants. It is now sold throughout the city. Most jasmine tea is produced in China's Fujian province from green tea leaves that are picked in spring and then placed close by or layered with fresh jasmine flowers in summer. The process can be repeated up to seven times until the tea is perfumed with the blooms' intense fragrance. Sometimes the tea leaves are rolled into tiny pearls that unfurl in hot water. Jasmine tea is delicious with dim sum or elegant cakes.

MOROCCAN MINT

JAPANESE GREEN

DARJEELING

LAPSANG SOUCHONG

MOROCCAN MINT

This aromatic herbal infusion is offered on the menus of all chic London restaurants and is favoured by fashion-conscious women who want a stylish, non-caffeinated drink. The best is found in Middle Eastern cafés, where fresh Moroccan mint leaves are infused in boiling water, then poured into tiny ornate cups and sweetened to taste with sugar.

JAPANESE GREEN

With the spread of Japanese restaurants in London, the taste for Japanese green teas has become a refreshing alternative to traditional British teas. Green teas are drunk at any time of the day. Many devotees seek out Japanese cups for savouring the exquisite flavour. The finest teas, Gyokura (Precious Dew), are grown under reed mats for 20 days in April to produce thick, soft, bright green leaves. After picking, the leaves are steamed, rolled, and dried to preserve their fresh taste. They need to be infused for only 2 minutes in hot, not boiling, water.

DARJEELING

The delicate flavour of Darjeeling tea makes it one of the most highly regarded black teas in Britain. It is favoured for afternoon tea with a slice of lemon or milk, but is drunk at any time. Grown high in the foothills of the Himalayas, Darjeeling has a light astringency. Many tea aficionados prefer the second flush for its slightly heavy, muscatel-like flavour. Specialty grocers such as Fortnum & Mason offer an amazing array of single-estate Darjeelings, including the floral-tasting first-flush Margaret's Hope and the unusual white Darjeeling from Castleton.

LAPSANG SOUCHONG

Londoners like tea with character, and Lapsang Souchong clearly falls into this category. This black China tea blend is easily recognisable by its tarry aroma and smoky taste. It is always served black or with lemon, usually in the afternoon and preferably with tiny smoked salmon sandwiches followed by a slice of walnut cake. The unique taste of Lapsang Souchong is partly the result of smoking the tea leaves after they have been dried. This characteristic makes the tea especially refreshing on a sultry summer day.

Since Roman times, Londoners have enjoyed the finest foods from around the world. Over the centuries, the city's great port on the Thames has been the destination of ships laden with delicacies, from Italian olives and New World chillies to Indian cardamom and West Indian pineapples.

DELICATESSENS

Walking across London, you can get a feel for the city's recent history by the type of delicatessen you find. Soho, for example, still has a few wonderful old-fashioned Italian delis, such as Camisa & Son (founded in 1929) in Old Compton Street and Lina Stores (1930) in Brewer Street, which marked the influx of Italian immigrants early in the twentieth century. As you stroll past the doors, you are tempted by the scent of salamis and Parmesan, and once inside you cannot resist buying fresh pumpkin ravioli or dipping into a sack of dried green flageolet beans.

When in Bayswater, you will notice the small delicatessens that cater to the Greeks who have been coming to worship at the Greek Orthodox cathedral of Aghia Sophia for well over a century. The Athenian Grocery in Moscow Road, like many of its neighbouring shops, brims in the summer with fresh grape leaves, green almonds, and sugar-dusted Turkish delight.

Wander through Marylebone and you will find smart delicatessens that reflect the tastes of the area's well-heeled residents. At Speck in Marylebone High Street, you will be offered a morsel of aged pecorino or marinated artichoke hearts wrapped in prosciutto to sample before you have even perused the fresh pasta, peppery olive oil, and marinated anchovy fillets. When you enter La Fromagerie in Moxon Street, you will want to linger over the incredible array of European cheeses before looking at the speciality foods such as French violet liqueur, Italian roast coffee beans, fresh Amalfi lemons, and Sri Lankan peppercorns. On the other side of Marylebone, in Great Portland Street, lies Villandry, with its astounding range of foods, such as luscious Danish pastries, dry-cured English bacon, chutneys and pickles, and myriad sea salts. Unlike older delis in London, these shops have tables where you can sip coffee or tea or enjoy a lunch of the specially made dishes, which you can also take home.

In the past, speciality grocers traditionally catered to the wealthy. In Roman times, London gourmands paid high prices for liquamen (fermented fish sauce), pine nuts, raisins, and olive oil imported from the Mediterranean. By the fifteenth century, canny medieval merchants were making their fortunes by importing costly sugar and expensive spices such as peppercorns, saffron, ginger, and cloves. As overseas trade grew, prices slowly dropped, and new imports were added to the array of edible delights.

Visiting a local deli will reveal more about a neighbourhood than any guidebook.

The Elizabethans, for example, were offered fresh oranges, candied citrus, and Parmesan cheese alongside spices, sugar, and dried fruits. By the eighteenth century, London was filled with specialist grocers and what were known as Italian warehouses. The latter were often started by Italian importers of olive oil, but they soon branched out to include such goods as rice, salt-preserved anchovies, dried macaroni, olives, and cocoa powder, as well as exotic ingredients like tamarind and spicy oriental sauces. Some merchants, such as

foie gras terrine, pig's cheek in Armagnac, and freshly baked Gascony breads and pies.

It is easy to lose a sense of London's vast size, and even its inhabitants regard the city as a collection of densely populated villages, each with its own character. Some areas, such as Chiswick, have well-established delis that understand the preferences of local residents and cater to them accordingly. Mortimer & Bennett in Turnham Green Terrace supplies Chiswickites with speciality foods, mainly French and Italian, such as fine

Walking across London, you can get a feel for the city's recent history and diversity by the type of delicatessens that you find.

Fortnum & Mason, began making potted beef, game in aspic, and other foods for customers to take home.

By the nineteenth century, the practice of purchasing prepared foods developed into another British institution: the hamper. On great social occasions such as Derby Day, members of London society would queue outside Fortnum & Mason in their carriages to collect picnic hampers of lobster salad and veal pies before driving down to the races at Epsom Downs. Hampers are now supplied by many delicatessens, including the other two grand food halls, Selfridges and Harrods.

Having retained the eclectic taste of their predecessors, Londoners consider it natural to use ingredients from around the world in their cooking. Most tend to patronise the shops nearest their work and home. Edgware Road locals, for instance, meander along the food aisles at the Lebanese delicatessen Green Valley in Upper Berkeley Street, considering what they might make with fruity-sour pomegranate syrup or dried broad beans. Shoppers passing through Smithfield stop off at the airy Comptoir Gascon in Charterhouse Street. Linked to the Michelin-starred Club Gascon, the shop sells its own

French conserves, pâtés, and more than thirty different oils. In areas that have been without delis, the opening of one often heralds social change. The arrival of Brindisa in Exmouth Market was a sign that Clerkenwell, with its converted loft spaces and bars, was becoming fashionable. The speciality at Brindisa is Spanish food, from salt cod and Iberico hams to superlative almonds, paprika, and saffron, and the deli now supplies many London restaurants and other shops.

Only one London delicatessen is dedicated to British food: A Gold in Brushfield Street near Liverpool Street Station. Situated in the smallest imaginable space, the shop is part of an eighteenth-century terrace and looks like an establishment out of the pages of a Charles Dickens novel. Here you can find delicious King's English pork pies, potted shrimps from Morecambe Bay, English apple juices, quince liqueur, local beer brewed in Hoxton, and London rooftop honey. Beekeeping has become a popular hobby among Londoners, who keep hives in tiny rooftop gardens. Some of the honey is collected and sold by the London Honey Company. Shoppers rarely leave A Gold without buying British sweets, whether toffee fudge or pink sugar mice.

British cheese making is enjoying an extraordinary renaissance, and London is the best place to sample some of the country's finest cheeses. Restaurants and shops offer a wonderful array of artisanal cheeses, from traditional favourites like creamy, savoury Stilton to the newest farmhouse varieties.

CHEESEMONGERS AND CHEESE

Life without cheese is inconceivable to most Londoners. For centuries, regional British cheeses were sold in London alongside such imports as Italian Parmesan. Some regions, such as the Midlands, Cheshire, and Somerset, became famous for the superb cow's milk cheeses they produce, namely Stilton, the renowned blue cheese from the Midlands; salty, white Cheshire; and tangy Cheddar from Somerset.

In the middle of the last century, however, the making of artisanal cheese fell into decline as government policies encouraged the mass production of inexpensive food and many superb farmhouse cheeses did not conform to supermarket demands for packaged, easy-to-slice cheese. While Londoners consoled themselves by buying French and Italian cheeses instead, occasionally, at Christmas

for example, they would seek out Cheddar or Stilton from a traditional cheesemonger, such as Paxton and Whitfield, which has sold cheese from its shop in Jermyn Street since 1797.

The situation changed dramatically in the early 1980s, when Randolph Hodgson, a maker of *fromage frais* and yoghurt, began to sell wonderful, but virtually unknown, British and Irish cheeses from his Neal's Yard Dairy in Covent Garden. Customers squeezed into the tiny shop overflowing with fragrant drums of Devonshire Beenleigh Blue, truckles of mature Appleby's Cheshire, and creamy rounds of Milleens from County Cork. The cheeses vanished as customers tasted the difference between farmhouse specialities and the mass-produced products sold in supermarkets. Soon Hodgson was driving around the country in search of artisanal

cheese makers. Knowing that they had an outlet for their products, cheese makers began to develop new varieties, such as Spenwood, a hard, mild sheep's milk cheese from Berkshire. Others produced new versions of continental cheeses, such as Cerney, an ash-coated fresh goat's cheese from Gloucestershire. Cheese-mongers and delis across the capital began selling regional cheeses again.

Another influence on Londoners' taste in cheese was La Fromagerie, opened by Patricia Michelson in Highbury in 1991. In 1995, with the aid of Eric Demelle, she began to perfect the French art of *affinage,* the process of maturing cheeses to further develop their taste and texture. The cheeses of La Fromagerie develop an intense, fruity taste and unctuous texture through *affinage.* Both Neal's Yard Dairy and La Fromagerie have opened second shops.

A ploughman's is a perfect pub lunch – fine cheese, fresh bread, and tangy pickle.

La Fromagerie

2-4 Moxon Street W1
Tel/Fax 020 7935 0341

OPEN EVERYDAY

Specialist Cheese Shop with
Wines, Selected Produce
& Café

Open all day serving
breakfast, lunch and
afternoon tea

Enjoy classic brunch fare
at weekends or a
la Fromagerie Picnic
in the park

STILTON

WIGMORE

DORSTONE

BERKSWELL

STILTON

Traditionally eaten at the end of a meal, and in greatest demand at Christmas, Stilton has an intense, savoury taste and creamy texture. Every Stilton-producing dairy follows its own recipe. Colston Bassett is still made in the traditional way in Nottinghamshire by ladling, rather than pouring, the cow's milk curds into a mould, which gives the cheese a particularly creamy texture. After the Stilton has matured a little, it is pierced with needles to allow air into it and encourage the growth of blue veins.

WIGMORE

The British love the understated, whether it is a wisp of a Philip Treacy-designed hat or a subtly fragrant, semisoft Wigmore cheese. The cheese is the creation of Anne Wigmore, an analytical cheese maker based in Berkshire, who set about creating new styles of cheese in the mid-1980s, including Waterloo and Spenwood. Wigmore is made from unpasteurised sheep's milk. To develop delicate flavour nuances, the curds are washed with water to dilute their acidic whey, then are left to ripen for up to six weeks, when the cheese acquires a bloomy rind.

DORSTONE

This lemony, soft, ash-coated goat's cheese is made by Charlie Westhead at Neal's Yard Creamery in Dorstone. With its delicate, fresh taste and crumbly, velvety texture, Dorstone is typical of the type of cheese Londoners like to eat during the summer months. Matured for only about ten days, this fresh cheese has a subtle acidity and flavour that needs no accompaniment other than some crusty bread or crisp radishes. It is perfect for impromptu picnics or lazy summer lunches.

BERKSWELL

It has become fashionable in London to offer a single cheese at the end of a meal with oatcakes and quince cheese. One of the best varieties for serving in this style is Berkswell, a West Midlands cheese with a floral taste and fudgy texture, created in 1989 by the Fletcher family. The Fletchers transform the unpasteurised milk from their East Friesland sheep into a new interpretation of a Caerphilly, usually made from lightly pressed and brine-soaked cow's milk curds. Berkswell is matured in basket-weave moulds, which imprint the exterior.

MRS KIRKHAM'S LANCASHIRE

STINKING BISHOP

BEENLEIGH BLUE

CHEDDAR

MRS KIRKHAM'S LANCASHIRE

For many years, traditionally made Lancashire was rarely seen outside the county; its crumbly texture and milky acidity were considered an acquired taste. In 1995, Randolph Hodgson, a cheesemonger in London, secretly entered Mrs. Kirkham's Lancashire cheese in the British Cheese Awards. It won Supreme Champion and became fashionable overnight. Mrs Kirkham, like her mother and grandmother before her, meticulously mixed the cow's milk curds over three days, then moulded and pressed them to make a golden, hard cheese wrapped in muslin.

STINKING BISHOP

Londoners are prone to daydreaming about rural life, particularly when eating Charles Martell's pungent semisoft Gloucestershire cheese. Some of the milk for the cheese comes from Martell's small herd of rare-breed Gloucester cows. The rind is washed with perry (pear cider), made from a rare local variety of pear called Stinking Bishop. The cheese develops a pale orange rind and a soft, creamy centre. The idea of saving an endangered cattle breed and a rare pear variety by making a delicious cheese makes Stinking Bishop appealing to Londoners.

BEENLEIGH BLUE

Beenleigh Blue was one of the first new British blue cheeses to arrive on the London restaurant scene in the 1980s. It is made from the milk of Dorset cross Friesland sheep by Sarie Cooper and Robin Congdon, founders of Ticklemore Cheese in Devon. Its sweet, nutty taste captivated London cheese eaters, who serve it with flowery dessert wine or crumble it into a watercress, pear, and walnut salad. Later, Ticklemore Cheese created a creamy, rich cow's milk blue cheese called Devon Blue and an intense-tasting goat's milk blue called Harbourne Blue.

CHEDDAR

Cheddar forms one of the ancient cornerstones of British cheese making. The name refers to a method of making cheese that originated around the Cheddar gorge in Somerset, but spread throughout the county. By the seventeenth century, local farmers were pooling their cow's milk to make vast truckles of Cheddar that could be matured for a couple of years. The best modern clothbound Cheddars vary, from the creamy Lincolnshire Poacher, which has a sweet buttery taste, to the crumbly, tangy Montgomery's Cheddar from Somerset.

On a warm summer evening, many a London street is filled with the murmuring of voices and the clinking of glasses. These are the sounds of the pub, an institution so integral to London life that few could imagine the city without it.

PUBS

The pub – or to be precise, the licensed public house – is there for everyone. It is a place to meet up for a quick drink after work, to enjoy an informal meal, or to quietly savour a pint of cool, aromatic bitter. The best pubs are warm and welcoming, providing a unique sense of egalitarianism. Today there are no rules about what you can drink. A gin and tonic, a non-alcoholic ginger beer, or a glass of wine are served as often as beer is. The British do not, as is so often asserted, drink beer warm. Instead, beer is drunk at the natural cellar temperature of 10–13°C (50–55°F), which allows the beer to continue maturing in its cask. As a result, it has a full flavour and a restrained natural carbonation.

London has around 5,500 pubs, which vary greatly in style from a homely mews pub with its cosy bar and quiet clientele to a hip-and-happening gastropub where people share their tables with strangers as they tuck into pumpkin and wild garlic risotto or chargrilled squid with tomatoes and olives. Gastropubs, a relatively recent phenomenon, began in 1991, when the Eagle opened in Farringdon Road, EC1. Most are started by young chefs who take over neglected pubs in the hopes of making their name – an endeavour that is far easier than investing in an expensive restaurant. The menu, often chalked up on a blackboard, tends to consist of simply made food using fresh, high-quality, seasonal ingredients: roast beetroot and fresh goat's cheese salad or salmon steaks with fennel, sorrel, and cucumber. A good wine list is usually offered along with the normal pub drinks. Gastropubs, such as the Coach & Horses in Ray Street, EC1, and the Oak in Westbourne Park Road, W11, are proving very popular with Londoners who crave relaxed local restaurants.

Although the British often worry that their pub culture is in decline, the reality is that modern pubs are following a long tradition of adapting to the needs of the day. Fifteenth-century London was filled with coaching inns, taverns, and ale houses. Each served a different purpose. Taverns, for example, were visited for their fine French wines and port. The latter was drunk in vast quantities whenever the wine trade was interrupted by war with France. One of the most famous taverns was Pontack's in Abchurch Lane, EC4, which served Château Haut-Brion clarets to customers including Sir Christopher Wren and Jonathan Swift. The tavern's modern descendant is the wine bar.

The flavour of a good beer, like wine, develops as it is sipped.

Coaching inns resembled hotels. Lying along the highways of Britain, they offered accommodation, food, drink, and stabling, as well as a good source of news from the mail coaches. Only one has survived in London – the George Inn in Borough High Street in Southwark, established in the 1540s during the reign of Henry VIII. Here you can linger over a fruity, dry Greene King Abbot Ale (from Suffolk), in much the same way one of the inn's earlier patrons, William Shakespeare, might have done with earlier brews. Southwark was a wild place in the

which by the beginning of the eighteenth century was sold to Londoners as Guinness.

Today, barely a handful of London breweries remain: Fuller, Smith & Turner (founded in 1845) in Chiswick, and Young & Co.'s Brewery in Wandsworth (1831) are the oldest; Pitfield Brewery (1980) in Hoxton and Meantime Brewing (2000) in Greenwich are the youngest. Many traditional London beers are "bitters", the correct term for a well-hopped ale imbued with a deep bitterness and a mild acidity. A mild ale is lightly hopped but has a full-bodied flavour.

London has around 5,500 pubs varying greatly in style from cosy bars to hip gastropubs where the food is the focus.

playwright's day. Situated beyond the reach of the city's ordinances, it was consequently awash with theatres, brothels, and bear pits. Coaching inns went into decline with the arrival of railways in the nineteenth century.

Ale houses are widely regarded as the direct ancestor of the public house. As their name implies, they served ale, a brew made from fermented grain. In the early fifteenth century, hops were added to this brew to help preserve it. From that time, ale (unhopped) became beer (hopped). Technically, the word *beer* refers to all drinks that have been fermented with grain and seasoned with hops. This term, however, is rarely applied to lager, porter, or stout.

Londoners have always drunk beers from all over England, including their own London brews. The latter were made with dark, malted barley, particularly from East Anglia, and aromatic Kentish, Herefordshire, and Worcestershire hops such Goldings or Fuggles. London Porter, a black, heavily hopped, and highly alcoholic beer, was created in London in the 1720s. It was exported to Ireland, where Arthur Guinness, a local brewer, produced his own version,

Different pubs offer different selections of beers. The choices are influenced by the brewery that owns the pub (independently owned pubs are known as freehouses). The Guinea, a small mews pub in Bruton Place in Mayfair, for instance, belongs to the Young's estate and is a good place to imbibe cask-conditioned, dry Young's Bitter or Young's Special. The Churchill Arms in Kensington Church Street is an example of a Fuller's pub. Customers can choose from an array of Fuller's beers including the flowery Chiswick Bitter, the more complex London Pride, or the deeper-flavoured Extra Special Bitter.

In contrast, the Greenwich Union is a modern pub on Royal Hill tied to Meantime Brewing, the brainchild of brew-master Alastair Hook. All the beers served at the pub come from his small brewery. Many are made in classic world styles, such as the delicate, fruity Cologne-style Kolsch and the light Bavarian wheat beer. Customers can request taster sets if they want to sample a few beers before deciding what to drink. Among the choices are the brewery's seasonals, including a light strawberry beer in summer and a chocolate stout in winter.

Just as the British have gained a renewed interest in native fish, it seems a cruel quirk of fate that the stocks from the ocean's larder have dwindled alarmingly from overfishing. This means that Londoners have to be far more selective about the fish they buy and where they buy it, resulting in an unprecedented and welcome focus on the provenance of seafood.

FISHMONGERS AND SEAFOOD

Fresh fish has long been an essential part of London life in both home kitchens and restaurants. In the eighteenth and nineteenth centuries, residents from all corners of society would sail down the Thames to taverns in Greenwich and Dagenham for whitebait banquets. Before the arrival of the railways in 1838, most of London's fish came from nearby Barking, home to the world's largest commercial fishing fleet. In the winter months, ice was harvested from the surrounding lowlands, which are now part of London, to preserve the summer catch.

At one time, every part of London had its own fishmonger, along with its own butcher, baker, and greengrocer. Today, fishmongers are an endangered species, as most people buy their seafood from supermarkets. Those businesses that survive owe their success to

sustained local custom and a reputation for selling superb seafood. Some, such as the traditional and popular Golborne Fisheries in North Kensington, sell an enormous range of tropical fish, as well as indigenous fish and shellfish. Mauritian owner George Ng bypasses the Billingsgate Fish Market and sources his supply directly from overseas or from the Plymouth ports. Others, such as the Fish Shop in Kensington Church Street, are small but smart new enterprises that bring in fresh fare daily from the Cornish coast.

Steve Hatt, an Islington institution, and Walter Purkis & Sons in Muswell Hill are renowned fishmongers who sell a wide array of fine fish, from wild sea bass and prawns to home-smoked mackerel and haddock. More centrally located, in Paddington Street, W1, is Blagden's, established in 1890 in a purpose-

built fishmonger's, where shoppers always find a seasonally changing display of British fish. Artfully arranged on the long marble slab might be Manx kippers one day and Scottish salmon the next.

In Marylebone High Street is the newest branch of FishWorks (another London location is the award-winning branch in Chiswick), a clever concept that combines a fishmonger's counter with an adjoining seafood restaurant. A recent addition to the London scene, FishWorks sells and serves impeccable fish, offering simple but rarely seen dishes such as fried herring melts (roe) on toast. Chef and food writer Mitchell Tonks, the enterprising owner, sources his fish direct from the morning's landings at Newquay, Padstow, Fowey, and St. Mawes in Cornwall. FishWorks also has an efficient home delivery service.

London fishmongers are blessed with access to some of the world's best seafood.

EELS

BROWN SHRIMPS

LOBSTER

COD

EELS

Inspiring appreciation and admira-
tion, this serpentine fish makes
its tenacious voyage from the
Sargasso Sea to London's rivers
and estuaries before it is caught
on its homeward journey to spawn.
The silvery adult eel is sold live
and is prised for its delicate but
richly flavoured flesh. The East
End's family-run pie-and-mash
shops have been preparing it two
ways for more than a century: cold
and jellied with malt vinegar and
bread and butter, and hot and
stewed with "liquor", a vivid green
parsley sauce. It is also excellent
smoked, served with horseradish.

BROWN SHRIMPS

Shrimps have a fond place in the
hearts of the British, with childhood
summer holidays spent paddling
in sand pools in an attempt to net
them. Not to be confused with the
larger prawns, these tiny delicacies
are grey when alive, but take on
a pinkish brown hue when briefly
boiled. Traditionally "potted" in
butter spiced with mace, nutmeg,
and cayenne, they are sublime
with crusty bread. Shrimps can
also be added to creamy sauces,
enveloped in mayonnaise, or
turned into a shrimp bisque.

LOBSTER

A quintessential ingredient of the
British "season" – Wimbledon
lawn tennis championships, the
Ascot races, and opera alfresco
at Glyndebourne – the king of crus-
tacea is caught between April and
October and sold live. Its dark blue
carapace and claws, which turn
scarlet when cooked, yield dense,
sweet white flesh, along with
creamy meat from the head. The
liver is used to enrich sauces, and
the precious coral (eggs) to make a
savoury butter. Lobster is served
cold, with herbed mayonnaise or
lemon, or hot, drizzled with melted
butter or a sophisticated sauce.

COD

Cod was once so prolific in North
Atlantic waters that a thriving
fishing port was located in the
Thames estuary. Stocks have
declined dramatically in recent
years, and cod is becoming a
scarce and expensive fish. As
green or grey as the sea, with
dappled lighter spots, this sleek
creature has pearly white flesh that
separates into firm, moist flakes,
making it suitable for poaching,
roasting, marinating, salting, and
drying, and perfect in a fish pie.
Deep-fried in golden batter, cod
forms half of Londoners' favourite
takeaway: fish and chips.

DOVER SOLE

CRAB

MACKEREL

WHITSTABLE OYSTERS

DOVER SOLE

Formerly a mainstay of classic English fish cookery, the exquisitely flavoured Dover sole, which thrives in the cold waters of the North Sea, has become an expensive luxury. A small flatfish with both eyes on one side of its head, it is half sepia and half cream, with dark patches. The fine flavour of its firm but delicate flesh is best eaten simply: grilled with a savoury butter, or accompanied by a delicate hollandaise sauce or beurre blanc. Sole is superb cooked on the bone or, once filleted, pan-fried, poached, or steamed.

CRAB

One of the finest crustaceans found in British waters, the brown crab is abundant and surprisingly inexpensive. The best specimens are caught far off shore, although traditional pots are still used in shallow waters. Often sold boiled, the crab is best presented as simply as possible: cold, with mayonnaise, lemon, and brown bread and butter. Fishmongers often sell dressed crab, separating white claw meat from brown body meat and mixing the latter with English mustard, chopped hard-boiled egg, and mayonnaise before piling the mixture back in the shell.

MACKEREL

This handsome fish has a svelte body cloaked in brilliant colours – shimmering metallic green-blue on top and silvery white on the underbelly. This oily fish spoils quickly and so is best eaten soon after being caught. The smaller specimens are best grilled or barbecued, while the larger are best stuffed and baked. All sizes benefit from being served with a piquant sauce or accompaniment to offset their richness. Gooseberry sauce is a classic choice, as is mustard butter. Mackerel is also delicious hot or cold smoked.

WHITSTABLE OYSTERS

In marked contrast to their current elevated status, these saltwater molluscs were once so prolific in Britain that they were bought by the barrel load and made into stews, soups, and fritters. Famed since the time of Dickens, the Whitstable oyster is opened just before eating with a special knife and consumed live to savour the briny juice and capture the elusive flavour. The raw oysters are sometimes dressed with shallot vinegar or lemon. When cooked – bathed in double cream, sprinkled with Parmesan, dotted with butter, and grilled – they are divine.

As dusk falls over London, the pace of life quickens in readiness for the evening ahead. Bartenders are busy replenishing their bars with fresh fruit, herbs, and ice. Then they turn the lights low. The stage is set. It's time to party.

BARS AND COCKTAILS

Stylish new bars open all the time, keen to attract Londoners who enjoy trying new places to have fun. Experimentation and rivalry are rife among "mixologists". This, along with the tolerant London lifestyle, attracts bartenders from around the world, and they, in turn, introduce new ingredients and fresh ideas, which further fuels the vibrant cocktail scene.

Until the early 1990s, the London bar scene was, to put it kindly, old-fashioned. If you wanted a classic cocktail, you went to a hotel bar such as the Cocktail Bar at Duke's Hotel in St. James's Place or the Library Bar in the Lanesborough Hotel at Hyde Park Corner. The latter became famous under the auspices of Salvatore Calabrese, who created various drinks, including the breakfast martini, made with lime marmalade, Cointreau, lemon juice, and plenty of gin.

By 1994, thirty-something Londoners were tiring of their nightclub culture. They wanted more relaxed environments that featured late-night music. At the same time, Dick Bradsell, London's supreme mixologist, was becoming well known for his superb cocktails. When Oliver Peyton opened the glamorous Atlantic Bar & Grill in 1996, he employed Bradsell to design the cocktail list and named one of the bars after him. Bradsell's influence was felt throughout the London cocktail scene as he created drinks menus for new bars. Many of London's best bartenders studied under him and tried to emulate his approach by sourcing the best and freshest ingredients for cocktails.

Within three years, the bar scene had taken off, with fashionistas drinking shots of fresh pineapple or watermelon vodka martinis at the minimalist Met Bar in the Metropolitan Hotel and media types sipping Dick Bradsell's Match Spring Punch at Jonathan Downey's Match EC1 in Clerkenwell.

Gradually, a London cocktail ethos is developing. The use of bottled juices and mixers is frowned on, and the best bars, such as the Townhouse in Beauchamp Place, SW3, Floridita in Wardour Street, W1, and Milk & Honey in Poland Street, W1, prepare their own juices and syrups, whether lime, ginger, or pineapple. Bartenders go to great lengths to source superlative spirits like Bramley & Gage quince liqueur or Havana Club three-year-old Cuban rum. Both contemporary and classic cocktails are subjected to rigorous competition and new cocktails are constantly evolving. Most important, London bartenders try to ensure that their customers' palates remain stimulated as the night drifts on.

Friends, music, and cocktails keep Londoners out until the early hours.

PIMM'S

OLD-FASHIONED

MOJITO

THE BRAMBLE

MATCH SPRING PUNCH

PIMM'S

In the 1840s, James Pimm created a bitter gin sling for his London restaurant. It proved so popular that he bottled it commercially as Pimm's Cup No. 1 in 1859. Londoners tend to drink it during the summer, preferably by the river or at garden parties. The bitter gin Pimm's mixture is poured into a jug, then is diluted with lemonade and ice and flavoured with lemon, borage flowers, and cucumber peel. Traditionally, the drink is served in a pint glass.

OLD-FASHIONED

Bourbon is enjoying a revival thanks to the classicist school of cocktails advocating beautifully made, traditional recipes. An orange slice, a maraschino cherry, bitters, and sugar are mixed in an old-fashioned glass, then bourbon, ice, and soda water are added.

MOJITO

Londoners love Cuba for its music, bars, and cigars. Consequently, London bartenders make lots of mojitos. They shake Havana rum with ice, bitters, soda water, fresh lime juice, mint, and sugar syrup before straining it over cracked ice.

THE BRAMBLE

English taste has been captured by this contemporary classic from renowned mixologist Dick Bradsell. The Bramble has an unusual musky flavour that comes from its *crème de mûre* (blackberry liqueur). It is made by shaking two parts dry Tanqueray No Ten gin, one part lemon juice, and a splash of sugar syrup with ice, then straining the mixture into a tumbler of crushed ice. After the drink is stirred, crème de mûre is drizzled over the ice so that the deep purple liqueur swirls ink-like into the liquid. The Bramble has become part of every London bartender's repertoire.

MATCH SPRING PUNCH

Concoct a long, bubbly, pink drink, and London women will love it, especially if accompanied by a plate of salty crisps. This drink goes by two names. The Match Bars claim it as their own, as it was originally put on the first Match Bar menu in Clerkenwell by its creator, Dick Bradsell. Other bars call it Russian Spring Punch, Bradsell's original name for the drink. Vodka, lemon juice, sugar syrup, crème de cassis, framboise, raspberries, and ice are shaken and strained into a tall glass with ice, then topped off with chilled Champagne.

FLAVOURED
COLLINS

CHAMPAGNE
COCKTAIL

VODKA
ESPRESSO

CAIPIRINHA

NEGRONI

FLAVOURED COLLINS

Two schools drive London cocktail fashion, the classicists and the experimentalists. The latter are influenced by Britain's top chefs. Flavoured collinses, made by experimentalists, are typical of British taste – combining superb gin with a seasonal ingredient such as elderflower or blackberry. The gooseberry-flavoured collins was created by London mixologist Nick Strangeway. Hendricks gin, gooseberry purée, fresh lemon juice, and lemon thyme syrup are mixed in a collins glass, topped with soda water, and garnished with lemon and lemon thyme.

CHAMPAGNE COCKTAIL

At certain times of year, especially at Christmas and New Year's, Londoners like to pull out all the stops at home and offer guests Champagne cocktails and smoked salmon canapés. The Bellini, a combination of fresh peach purée, peach liqueur, and *prosecco,* may be more popular in summer, but it lacks the Champagne cocktail's sophisticated and subtle bitterness, a flavour that comes from a few drops of Angostura bitters soaked into a single sugar cube. A splash of good Cognac, such as Remy Martin, is added to the flute, followed by dry Champagne.

VODKA ESPRESSO

Londoners have a taste for coffee and alcohol. Combine them in a cocktail, and you have a classic London wake-up drink. This is exactly what Dick Bradsell did in the 1990s when he devised his ice-cold vodka espresso, otherwise known as the Pharmaceutical Stimulant, for the über-hip bar at the now defunct Pharmacy in Notting Hill, which was co-owned and designed by artist Damien Hirst. Vodka espresso is often made with Illy espresso and Finlandia vodka, plus a touch of Kahlúa, then is shaken with ice and strained into a glass.

CAIPIRINHA

Based on *cachaca,* a Brazilian spirit made from fresh sugar cane, the caipirinha is a delicious cocktail that takes time to mix properly. Tempered with fresh lime, brown sugar, and ice, the fresh-tasting result is worth the wait.

NEGRONI

London bartenders like nothing better than to sip a bittersweet Florentine Negroni after hours and mull over the evening's events. Made with vermouth, Campari, and Tanqueray gin, it is served in a cold old-fashioned glass, garnished with flamed orange peel.

Word spreads fast when a good artisanal bakery opens in London. Locals, as well as customers from further afield, soon show up at the door, eager to try the tempting new selection of pastries and breads. Their biggest challenge is deciding what to order.

BAKERIES

London is such an international city that it is possible to buy every conceivable type of bread, from fresh sourdough bread at Poilâne in Elizabeth Street, SW1, to rosemary, raisin, or sea salt bread at & Clarke's in Kensington Church Street. The bakeries reflect the city's extraordinary ethnic diversity, each catering to local tastes by making Italian *pugliese*, Turkish flat *pide*, French *fougasse*, soft white English baps, or Jewish rye and challah. The most notable bakers experiment in a way they could not elsewhere in the world because Londoners are often happy to try anything new and are accustomed to being introduced to innovative ideas and unfamiliar ingredients.

Dan Lepard is the most talked-about baker in Britain. He has worked for some of London's foremost restaurants and chefs, including Giorgio Locatelli at Zafferano and Locanda Locatelli, and his influence has spread. His book, *The Handmade Loaf,* has positioned him at the forefront of the British bread revival. Restaurant critic Fay Maschler has described him as "the bread supremo".

Baker & Spice in Denyer Street, SW3, and Elizabeth Street, SW1, where Lepard once worked, is a purveyor of irresistible cakes, outstanding breads, and extraordinary pastries and tarts. Owner Gail Stephens, who is fiercely passionate about her baked goods, has rightly won critical acclaim. She sells a huge variety of breads, including a *pane con noci* that is so packed with walnuts and raisins it is almost a cake, a sensational garlic bread studded with whole caramelised cloves, and a traditional British milk knot.

Restaurateur Sally Clarke's bakery, & Clarke's, prides itself on using the highest-quality ingredients – without artificial colours, preservatives, or improvers – in the fresh breads and pastries on display early each morning. Every night, the bakers hand-shape and bake more than two thousand loaves, which are sent to some of the top restaurants, shops, and hotels in central London. The inventive range includes an oatmeal honeypot with organic oats, baked in a flowerpot shape; a loaf in the form of ears of maize; and narrow breadsticks with dried figs and fennel seeds.

Legendary across the city for its diversity of handmade breads – from eastern Europe, Ireland, the Mediterranean, and North America – De Gustibus is best known for its six-day sourdough loaf. Other temptations include pumpernickel, Polish rye, Irish wheat loaf, and tortino, a Tuscan focaccia filled with vegetables and cheese.

Artisanal bakers approach their craft with regard for both tradition and innovation.

Originally from Cornwall, the Cornish pasty was first conceived as a lunchtime snack for local tin miners. The crimped edge of the pastry parcel acted as a handle and was later discarded after being blackened by the miner's fingers. So large were the pasties that one end could contain a savoury filling, the other a sweet one – making a complete, portable meal.

Questions of authenticity

Bakers throughout the country make Cornish pasties, although the "authentic" method is the subject of hot debate. Classic pasties combine diced beef with onions, sliced potatoes, and root vegetables such as turnips or carrots. Some cooks claim that the order in which the ingredients are layered is crucial. Others assert that the position of the crimp – on the top or on the side – is what determines authenticity. They all agree on one point: a pasty must be made from raw ingredients.

History of the pasty

Many Cornish folk will tell you that a genuine pasty can be made only with shortcrust, while others advocate using a rough puff pastry. Either way, in times gone by, the pastry needed to be sufficiently strong to withstand a miner's descent into a mineshaft and thick enough to provide insulation for the hot filling until the miner could snatch a moment from his toil to eat.

Lest his pasty be confused with another miner's, his wife would mark it with a knife, carving his initials into the left-hand side. This was especially useful if the miner wanted to save a corner for later, or to placate the Knockers, the "little people" of the mines, who were thought to cause mischief.

Surprisingly for a coastal region, fish rarely found its way into the Cornish pasty. The more superstitious among the fishermen thought it bad luck even to take a pasty on board their boat, regardless of its contents. Today, the Cornish pasty has joined the fast-food brigade, with fillings as outré as crab, pork and apple, lamb and mint, cheese and smoked bacon – and even a spicy chicken balti.

Making Cornish pasties

MAKING THE PASTRY Flour and salt are sifted into a bowl, then fat – traditionally lard – is rubbed in until the mixture resembles fine breadcrumbs. Ice-cold water is then added little by little to make a soft dough. The dough is then chilled.

MAKING THE FILLING Beef is the traditional filling for pasties. It is first trimmed, then finely chopped (never minced). Finely sliced potatoes, diced onions, and root vegetables, such as carrots, swedes, or turnips, are then added to the beef along with chopped fresh thyme, salt, and pepper.

FORMING THE PASTIES The pastry is rolled out and cut into rounds. The filling is then arranged down the centre of each round, and the edge is brushed with beaten egg. The opposite sides of the round are folded over the top of the filling and crimped together to form a wavy seam. The pasties are then brushed with egg.

BAKING THE PASTIES The pasties are baked in a 200°C (392°F) oven for 20 minutes. The heat is then reduced to 180°C (356°F), and they are baked for 40 minutes, or until golden brown.

AFTERNOON TEA

The scent of Earl Grey tea and a plate of warm buttered

scones anticipates one of London's much-loved pleasures.

While the formalities of tea are observed in some elegant hotels, most Londoners approach this centuries-old ritual with a relaxed attitude suited to the demands of urban life. Nevertheless, traditional savouries such as scones flecked with ham and farmhouse cheese, and delicate egg sandwiches spiced with cress, are still welcome accompaniments to freshly brewed tea. Classic mince pies and contemporary versions of fairy cakes are among the delicious array of cakes on tea menus. Nowadays, the drink of choice might be a cup of coffee, enjoyed in one of the city's many cafés with a slice of lemon drizzle cake.

CHOCOLATE FAIRY CAKES

Fairy cakes have been enjoying a renaissance in recent years. Instead of buying a large cake to celebrate a birthday or an anniversary, Londoners often opt for these diminutive sponge cakes, whether vanilla, almond, lemon, orange, or chocolate. Once iced they may be decorated with tiny sweets, candied organic flower petals, or even wisps of edible gold leaf. Traditionally, such cakes are served for tea or with morning coffee. London mums bake vast quantities to sell at school fêtes; the competition ensures a beautiful presentation.

1 Preheat the oven to 160°C (325°F). Line 24 patty tins or shallow bun tins with paper cake cases or grease the tins with butter.

2 In a small saucepan, combine the chocolate, milk, and half of the brown sugar. Set over a low heat and stir until the chocolate is melted. Remove from the heat and stir in the ground espresso. Set aside to cool.

3 Using an electric mixer, beat the butter with the remaining brown sugar for 5 minutes or until light and fluffy. Add the egg and beat until it is incorporated. Sift the flour, baking powder, and cocoa powder into a separate bowl, then add to the butter mixture and beat for about 2 minutes or until well mixed.

4 Using a metal spoon, fold in the cooled chocolate mixture. Divide the mixture among the tins. Bake for 15–20 minutes or until a skewer inserted into the centre of a cake comes out clean. Remove them from the oven and transfer to a wire rack to cool.

5 To make the icing, put the butter, chocolate, and golden syrup in a bowl set over a saucepan of simmering water. Heat gently until melted and smooth, stirring constantly. Allow to cool, then, using an electric mixer, beat until thick and fluffy.

6 Spread a thick layer of icing over the top of each cake. Leave to set for 1 hour before serving. If you like, decorate with finely grated white chocolate. The cakes can be kept in an airtight container at room temperature for up to 2 days.

Serve with Earl Grey or Darjeeling tea.

60 g (2 oz) good dark chocolate, coarsely chopped

4 tablespoons whole milk

200 g (7 oz) soft light brown sugar

2 teaspoons very finely ground espresso

60 g (2 oz) unsalted butter, at room temperature

1 medium egg, beaten

115 g (4 oz) plain flour

½ teaspoon baking powder

1 tablespoon cocoa powder

FOR THE ICING

85 g (3 oz) unsalted butter

75 g (2½ oz) good dark chocolate, coarsely chopped

1½ teaspoons golden syrup

Finely grated white chocolate, to decorate (optional)

Makes 24 cakes

Chocolate shops

Londoners have a strong sense of style, and for certain occasions only a smart box of chocolates will do. Charbonnel et Walker and Fortnum & Mason were the best choices for years, the former supplying the royal family since 1875. Charbonnel's became famous for its chocolate-dipped violet and rose creams.

For years, nothing challenged the old order in Britain. Then, in 1983, Chantal Coady opened Rococo, a glamorous chocolate boutique. She was passionate about selling the finest chocolate: white truffles infused with cardamom, and chocolate bars flavoured with delicacies such as geranium and sea salt.

In 2000, L'Artisan du Chocolat set up a modest stall at Borough Market and started to sell handmade couture chocolates. Rather than containing traditional chocolate flavourings found in France, the ganaches were infused with innovative ingredients such as black cardamom and Moroccan mint. The company started supplying top British chefs such as Gordon Ramsay before opening a shop. Londoners can now slip into the chic environment whenever they need to savour a rosemary or red wine chocolate.

HOT CROSS BUNS

On Good Friday during the nineteenth century, cries of "one-a-penny, two-a-penny, hot cross buns" were heard in the streets of London as vendors sold sweet buns marked with a cross. The spicy fruited buns originated in Tudor times, and by the reign of Elizabeth I they were so popular that their sale was restricted to the serious observances of burials, Christmas, and Good Friday. What fed their appeal was Londoners' taste for expensive imports such as sugar, spices, and dried fruits. Today, although hot cross buns are mainly associated with Good Friday, they are eaten throughout much of the year.

120 ml (4 fl oz) whole milk

300 g (10 oz) strong (bread) flour, or as needed

2 tablespoons caster sugar

½ teaspoon *each* fine sea salt and ground cinnamon

¼ teaspoon *each* ground mace and freshly grated nutmeg

Good pinch *each* ground cloves and ground allspice (optional)

25 g (scant 1 oz) cold unsalted butter, diced

1 teaspoon easy-blend yeast

60 g (2 oz) *each* sultanas, currants, and chopped candied peel

1 medium egg, beaten

FOR THE PASTRY CROSSES

60 g (2 oz) plain flour

15 g (½ oz) unsalted butter, diced

1 teaspoon caster sugar

FOR THE GLAZE

2 tablespoons whole milk

1½ tablespoons granulated sugar

Makes 6 buns

1 In a small saucepan, warm the milk to 40°C (105°F). Remove from the heat and set aside.

2 Sift the flour into a large bowl. Stir in the sugar, salt, cinnamon, mace, nutmeg, cloves, and allspice (if using). Using your fingertips, rub the butter into the flour until the mixture resembles breadcrumbs. Mix in the yeast and then the sultanas, currants, and candied peel. Make a well in the centre and stir in the egg and enough of the warm milk to form a soft dough. It should not be too sticky: if it clings to your fingers, add a little more flour.

3 Turn the dough out on to a lightly floured work surface. Knead for about 10 minutes or until smooth and elastic. Return the dough to the bowl, cover with cling film, and leave in a warm place for 3–5 hours or until the dough has risen by a third. The timing depends on the temperature of the kitchen.

4 Lightly oil a baking sheet. Turn the risen dough out on to a lightly floured work surface. Knead for 1 minute, then divide into 6 equal pieces. Shape each piece into a neat ball and place on the baking sheet, flattening each ball slightly. Cover lightly with cling film and leave to rise for about 45 minutes or until the dough is very puffy.

5 Preheat the oven to 200°C (400°F). To make the pastry crosses, sift the flour into a small bowl. Using your fingertips, rub in the butter until the mixture forms fine crumbs. Mix in the sugar. Stir in 1 tablespoon cold water to make a firm dough. Turn

the dough out on to a lightly floured work surface and roll out to a rectangle about 20 x 5 cm (8 x 2 inches) and 3 mm (⅛ inch) thick. Cut into 12 strips, each one about 10 cm (4 inches) long and 5 mm (¼ inch) wide. For each bun, brush 2 strips with a little water and arrange, damp side down, in a cross on the top of the bun. Bake for 15 minutes or until golden brown.

6 Meanwhile, make the glaze. Put the milk and sugar in a small saucepan over a low heat and cook, stirring occasionally, for 5 minutes. Increase the heat to high and boil for about 30 seconds or until the mixture becomes syrupy. Remove from the heat.

7 When the buns are baked, transfer to a wire rack and immediately brush with the hot glaze. Serve the buns warm or at room temperature. They can also be split open and toasted.

Serve with Assam or Darjeeling tea or with coffee.

Note: The buns can be wrapped tightly in cling film and frozen for up to 1 month. Before serving, thaw the buns at room temperature for about 1 hour, then warm through in a preheated 180°C (350°F) oven for 4–5 minutes.

EGG AND CRESS SANDWICHES

Tea was first served in Britain in 1658 at the Sultaness Head, a coffeehouse in Sweetings Rents near London's Royal Exchange. One hundred years passed before afternoon tea became established. It initially featured thin, buttered slices of bread, but by the nineteenth century, the centrepiece was dainty sandwiches filled with eggs, cucumber, or watercress. Peppery mustard and cress – the seeds of the two sprouted together to the two-leaf stage – is the traditional partner for an egg mayonnaise filling.

1 Bring a small saucepan of water to the boil over a moderately high heat. Carefully lower the eggs into the water, return the water to the boil, and boil the eggs for 10 minutes. Immediately plunge the eggs into iced water. When the eggs are cool enough to handle, peel them under cold running water, being sure to remove every speck of shell. Pat the eggs dry with a tea towel.

2 Place the eggs in a bowl and finely mash with a fork or potato masher. Add the mayonnaise and mash again. Season to taste with salt, black pepper, and cayenne.

3 Spread 2 slices of bread with the egg mixture, dividing it evenly. Arrange the snipped cress on the egg mixture. Top with the remaining bread slices, pressing firmly. Using a serrated knife, remove the crusts from each sandwich, then cut into 3 fingers or 4 triangles.

4 If not serving the sandwiches immediately, cover tightly with cling film and keep in the fridge for up to 2 hours.

Serve with Darjeeling or Earl Grey tea.

2 medium eggs

1 tablespoon mayonnaise

Fine sea salt and freshly ground black pepper

Pinch of cayenne pepper, or to taste

4 thin slices good-quality white bread

1 punnet mustard and cress

Makes 2 servings

The sandwich

For the last 150 years, sandwiches have fuelled Londoners' workdays. At lunchtime, office workers pour into cafés to buy their favourite sarnie. Classic fillings such as smoked salmon or cheese and pickle are still popular. Among recent trends are sandwiches with Thai chicken or prawns and rocket.

John Montagu, fourth Earl of Sandwich, is said to have invented the sandwich around 1760 while gambling. Keen not to be distracted from his game, he ordered cold beef served between slices of buttered bread. Within two years, the fashionable elite were eating "the Sandwich". By the mid-1800s, its consumption had spread throughout London society. Watercress sandwiches were served for breakfast, cucumber for tea, and jam at picnics. Theatre patrons bought ham and mustard sandwiches from street vendors, and the wealthy dined on dainty veal sandwiches.

Sandwiches have always invited experimentation, but few rivalled Mrs Sawbridge's creation two hundred years ago. She made and then scornfully ate a delicate sandwich containing a hundred-pound note given her by an admirer.

CHEESE AND HAM SCONES

A proper afternoon tea can still be sampled in most of London's grand hotels, such as the elegant Palm Court at the Ritz and the wood-panelled Drawing Room at the Connaught in Mayfair. It always includes a savoury dish or two, for example, sandwiches, anchovy toasts, crumpets, or scones. Although scones are commonly sweet, studded with sultanas and served with clotted cream, many savoury varieties exist, one of the most popular being cheese and ham. The best Cheddar, tangy, nutty, and rich, is made by small artisanal dairies such as Keen's or Montgomery's in Somerset.

250 g (9 oz) plain flour

1 teaspoon cream of tartar

½ teaspoon bicarbonate of soda

Pinch of fine sea salt

60 g (2 oz) cold unsalted butter, diced, plus more for serving

85 g (3 oz) mature Cheddar cheese, finely grated

115 g (4 oz) ham, finely diced

150 ml (5 fl oz) whole milk

1 medium egg

Makes 12 scones

1 Preheat the oven to 220°C (425°F). Lightly oil a baking tray.

2 Sift the flour, cream of tartar, bicarbonate of soda, and salt into a bowl. Rub in the butter until the mixture forms coarse crumbs. Alternatively, place the sifted dry ingredients in a food processor, add the butter, and pulse 4 or 5 times until the mixture forms coarse crumbs; return to the bowl. Using a fork, stir in the cheese and ham. In a small bowl, beat the milk into the egg, then add to the flour mixture. Stir just until a rough, soft dough forms.

3 Turn the dough out on to a floured work surface and lightly knead for about 1 minute or until it clings together and is soft and puffy. Gently roll out into a round about 2 cm (¾ inch) thick. Dust a 5.5 cm (2¼ inch) round biscuit cutter with flour and, using a quick, sharp motion, cut out scones as close together as possible. Gather the scraps of dough and knead briefly together, then roll out and cut additional scones. Place the scones 4 cm (1½ inches) apart on the prepared baking tray.

4 Bake for about 10 minutes or until golden brown. Serve hot or leave to cool to room temperature on a wire rack. Serve with butter. The scones should be eaten the day they are baked, or can be frozen for up to 2 weeks in an airtight container.

Serve with Darjeeling, Earl Grey, or Lapsang Souchong tea.

LEMON AND LAVENDER DRIZZLE CAKE

Londoners like nothing better than enjoying a cup of coffee or tea and cake in a café, while watching the world pass by. Midmorning and midafternoon are the favourite times for such indulgences, and many cafés offer outdoor seating much of the year. While some Londoners prefer French confections, others are fond of simple English cakes like this lavender cake with the fresh, floral taste of the English countryside, embellished with an old-fashioned drizzle icing. The best source for pesticide-free lavender is your own garden or a friend's.

1   Preheat the oven to 180°C (350°F). Generously butter a 23 x 13 cm (9 x 5 inch) loaf tin.

2   Strip the flowers from the lavender sprigs. Place in a food processor and add the caster sugar, butter, lemon zest, and salt. Process for 2–3 minutes or until pale and fluffy. Transfer to a large bowl. Add the eggs one at a time alternately with the flour, beating well with a wooden spoon after each addition. Gently stir in the ground almonds and lemon juice.

3   Spoon the mixture into the prepared tin and smooth the top. Bake for 10 minutes. Reduce the oven temperature to 165°C (325°F) and bake for a further 50–55 minutes or until a skewer inserted into the centre comes out clean. Remove from the oven and allow to rest in the tin on a wire rack for 5 minutes. Run a table knife around the inside edge of the tin and turn the cake out on to the rack. Place right side up and leave to cool.

4   Meanwhile, make the icing. Sift the icing sugar into a bowl. Using a wooden spoon, stir in the lemon juice, a few drops at a time. The icing should be thick but spreadable. If the icing is too stiff, add a few more drops of lemon juice.

5   Using a knife and dipping it in hot water if it becomes too sticky, spread the icing over the top of the cooled cake, making sure that it drips down the sides. Leave to stand for about 1 hour or until the icing is set. Decorate with fresh lavender flowers, if you like. The cake will keep, stored in an airtight container without the fresh flower decoration, for up to 3 days.

8 sprigs pesticide-free fresh lavender flowers (see note) or 1 teaspoon finely chopped, pesticide-free fresh lavender leaves, plus flowers to decorate (optional)

250 g (9 oz) caster sugar

225 g (8 oz) unsalted butter, at room temperature

Finely grated zest of 2 lemons

Pinch of fine sea salt

4 medium eggs

60 g (2 oz) sifted plain flour

175 g (6 oz) ground almonds

4 tablespoons fresh lemon juice

FOR THE ICING

175 g (6 oz) icing sugar

Juice of ½ large lemon, or as needed

Makes 8–10 servings

London coffeehouses

A love of good coffee helped shape modern London. In the early seventeenth century, British travellers to Turkey developed such a liking for arabica coffee beans that they imported them on their return. The craze for coffee soon took hold of fashionable society, and in 1652 the first of the city's coffeehouses was opened in St Michael's Alley by Pasqua Rosee, a Croatian native. At their peak there were hundreds of coffeehouses in London, and the coffeehouse became a place where men of all classes could meet, talk, and circulate uncensored news sheets. Business deals discussed over coffee created the insurance giant, Lloyd's of London, and some of the city's most exclusive gentlemen's clubs are direct descendants of coffeehouses.

After two hundred years, coffeehouses began to decline, partly because they became quite popular with characters of ill repute and partly because tea had superseded coffee in popularity. Tea, grown in the British colonies, was less expensive than coffee. Today, however, coffee is more popular than ever, and you can find cafés and coffee shops in great profusion all over London.

MINCE PIES

A centuries-old British speciality, mince pies start appearing in London shops about six weeks before Christmas. In medieval times, the mincemeat filling of dried fruits, candied peel, and apples also contained beef. Suet, which later took the place of beef, is often omitted from contemporary versions, like the one here. This recipe makes more mincemeat than you will need for the pies. Since its flavour improves with age, the extra can be stored for future use – it will keep for up to six months. The pies are perfect with a cup of tea and also delicious served with mulled wine for festive occasions.

FOR THE MINCEMEAT

1 kg (2¼ lb) cooking apples

175 ml (6 fl oz) cider

200 g (7 oz) soft dark brown sugar

250 g (9 oz) *each* dried currants and raisins

60 g (2 oz) glacé cherries, roughly chopped

Grated zest and juice of 1 lemon and 1 orange

½ teaspoon ground cinnamon

Pinch of freshly grated nutmeg

Small pinch of ground cloves

4 tablespoons brandy

FOR THE PASTRY

210 g (7½ oz) plain flour

Pinch of fine sea salt

85 g (3 oz) cold unsalted butter, diced

1 medium egg yolk

3–4 tablespoons cold water

1 tablespoon whole milk

2 tablespoons granulated sugar

Makes 12 mince pies

1 To make the mincemeat, peel, core, and grate the apples. Combine the cider and brown sugar in a large non-metallic saucepan. Set over a moderate heat and cook, stirring occasionally, until the sugar has dissolved. Add the apples, currants, raisins, cherries, lemon and orange zest and juice, cinnamon, nutmeg, and cloves. Cook, stirring constantly, for about 5 minutes or until the mixture comes slowly to the boil. Reduce the heat to low, partly cover, and simmer gently for about 1 hour or until a thick, soft paste is formed. Uncover, increase the heat to moderate, and cook briskly, stirring frequently, for about 10 minutes or until all the liquid has evaporated. Stir in the brandy. If not using the mincemeat immediately, pack into hot sterilised jars. When cool, store in a cool, dark place.

2 To make the pastry, sift the flour and salt into a bowl. Rub in the butter until the mixture forms coarse crumbs. Alternatively, place the sifted dry ingredients in a food processor, add the butter, and pulse 4 or 5 times until the mixture forms coarse crumbs; return to the bowl. Using a fork, stir in the egg yolk and enough of the cold water to form a rough dough. Turn the dough out on to a lightly floured work surface and lightly knead for about 1 minute or until smooth. Shape the dough into a disc 2 cm (¾ inch) thick and wrap in cling film. Put in the fridge to chill for at least 30 minutes or up to 12 hours.

3 Preheat the oven to 180ºC (350°F). Lightly butter 12 individual tart tins about 6 cm (2½ inches) in diameter. On a lightly floured work surface, roll out two-thirds of the pastry dough into a round 3 mm (⅛ inch) thick. Using a 7.5 cm (3 inch) cutter, cut out 12 circles. Gather the scraps of dough and roll out with the remaining dough, dusting the dough with flour as needed to keep it from sticking to the work surface. Using a 6 cm (2½ inch) round or star-shaped cutter, cut out 12 shapes.

4 Line each prepared tin with a large circle of dough. Fill with about 1 tablespoon of mincemeat. Brush the edges of a small pastry circle with milk, place milk side down on top of the filling, and press the edges together lightly to seal. If using stars, brush the tips of the stars with milk, place on top of the filling, and press the tips into the edges to seal. Prick the top of each pie with a sharp knife, then brush with milk and sprinkle with granulated sugar.

5 Bake the pies for about 20 minutes or until the pastry is golden. Remove from the tins and leave to cool on a wire rack. Serve the pies warm or at room temperature. They can be stored in an airtight tin for up to 2 days.

Serve with Darjeeling or Earl Grey tea or mulled wine.

STARTERS

Global influences and a taste for innovation are the foundation for

starters on both restaurant menus and the tables of home cooks.

Londoners like to experiment when making starters and canapés. The distinctive flavours of cuisines from around the world are married with local ingredients to make Thai meatballs with a sweet chilli and lemongrass sauce, or a Middle Eastern mezze made up of houmous, tabbouleh, and crisp vegetables. At parties, elegant blini with smoked salmon and crème fraîche, colourful vegetable crisps, or spicy samosas might be offered to guests. Restaurant diners regularly order a starter or two in place of a main course, and home cooks might prepare a cheese tart with a salad for a light lunch.

BLINI WITH SMOKED SALMON AND CRÈME FRAÎCHE

Blini with smoked salmon or caviar have long been popular in the City of London, the capital's prosperous financial district. The area, a mere square mile, is renowned for its expensive tastes, which often influence chefs working elsewhere in the capital. Blini, for example, are now regularly found on menus throughout London. Buckwheat flour adds a distinctive nutty taste to the pancakes, but since it can be hard to find, it can be replaced with wholemeal flour. Some of the finest smoked salmon comes from Scotland and Ireland, where wild Atlantic salmon is skilfully smoked to bring out its sweet flavour.

1 To make the blini, warm a large bowl by filling it with hot water, emptying it, and wiping it dry. Combine the plain and buckwheat flours and yeast in the bowl. In a small saucepan over a moderate heat, warm the milk just until small bubbles appear round the edge of the pan; do not let it come to the boil. Slowly pour the milk into the dry ingredients, beating constantly with a wooden spoon to form a smooth batter. Cover with cling film and leave to rise in a warm place for about 2 hours or until doubled in bulk.

2 Beat together the egg yolk, salt, melted butter, and soured cream. Add to the risen batter and, using the wooden spoon, beat until combined. In another bowl, whisk the egg white until stiff peaks form. Using a metal spoon, fold into the batter. Cover with cling film and leave to stand for 30 minutes.

3 Preheat the oven to its lowest setting. In a large non-stick frying pan over a moderately high heat, warm 1 teaspoon of the sunflower oil. When it is hot, drop a few tablespoonfuls of batter into the pan, leaving 4 cm (1½ inches) of space between the blini.

Cook for about 2 minutes or until the blini are puffed and golden brown and tiny bubbles appear on the surface. Using a palette knife, turn the blini and cook for 2 minutes on the other side or until golden brown. Transfer to an ovenproof plate and keep warm in the oven. Continue making more blini in the same way, using 1 teaspoon of oil for each batch. You should make about 16 blini in all.

4 Divide the blini among individual plates. To serve, place a heaping tablespoonful of crème fraîche on each plate, setting it partially on the warm blini. Divide the salmon among the plates, setting it on top of the blini. Garnish each plate with chives, a light grinding of pepper (if using), and a lemon wedge. Serve at once.

Serve with a creamy white Burgundy or Blanc des Blancs Champagne.

FOR THE BLINI

75 g (2½ oz) plain flour

45 g (1½ oz) buckwheat flour

½ teaspoon easy-blend yeast

120 ml (4 fl oz) whole milk

1 medium egg, separated

Pinch of fine sea salt

15 g (½ oz) unsalted butter, melted

1 tablespoon soured cream

4 teaspoons sunflower oil or clarified unsalted butter (see page 185)

TO SERVE

175 g (6 oz) crème fraîche

400 g (14 oz) thinly sliced smoked salmon

6 fresh chives, coarsely snipped

Freshly ground pepper (optional)

4 lemon wedges

Makes 4 servings

POTTED SHRIMPS

This classic starter is traditionally made with tiny, sweet brown shrimps from Morecambe Bay, but larger prawns, cut into small pieces, can also be used. The recipe here follows the eighteenth-century method of seasoning the peeled shrimps with ground mace and cayenne pepper and simmering them very gently in clarified butter before sealing them in ramekins (originally little china pots were used). Londoners like to eat potted shrimps in classic British restaurants such as Simpson's-in-the-Strand or the Paternoster Chop House in Paternoster Square, EC4.

400 g (14 oz) unsalted butter, clarified (see page 185)

500 g (1 lb 2 oz) cooked peeled brown shrimps

¼ teaspoon ground mace

¼ teaspoon cayenne pepper

Buttered hot toast to serve

2 lemons, cut into wedges, to serve

6 fresh chives, coarsely snipped, to garnish (optional)

Makes 4 servings

1 Pour 250 ml (8 fl oz) of the clarified butter into a small non-metallic saucepan. Pat the shrimps dry with kitchen paper and remove any tiny pieces of shell clinging to them. If the shrimps are not really tiny, cut them into 5 mm (¼ inch) pieces. Add the shrimps, mace, and cayenne to the butter in the saucepan. Set over a low heat. If the shrimps are cold, the butter will thicken. Stir until the butter melts, then very gently cook for about 5 minutes or until the shrimps are hot and the spices have infused the butter.

2 Divide the shrimps and spiced butter among 4 ramekins, firmly pressing down on the shrimps with a metal spoon. Place in the fridge to chill for about 4 hours or until the butter is set.

3 In a small saucepan over a low heat, warm the remaining clarified butter just until it melts; don't allow it to become hot. Pour the butter into the ramekins, dividing evenly. Chill for a further 2 hours (or overnight) until cold and set.

4 Serve the potted shrimps with hot toast and lemon wedges. Garnish with the chives, if you like.

Serve with a buttery white Burgundy such as Chassagne-Montrachet or Pouilly-Fuissé.

Note: If you leave the potted shrimps to set overnight, the flavours will become more developed. This starter should be eaten no later than 1 day after it is made.

VEGETABLE CRISPS

Having a drink after work is integral to London life. Most Londoners head to a local pub or bar for a few hours of socialising before dinner. Salty snacks are an essential accompaniment to the drinks. Most pubs sell packets of crisps or nuts, but stylish bars serve their own vegetable crisps, bread sticks, and marinated olives. The crisps are made from finely sliced root vegetables, such as potatoes, parsnips, and celeriac, then are tossed in fine sea salt, but they can also be flavoured with a dusting of chilli powder or chopped fresh thyme.

1 Using a mandolin or sharp knife, cut the parsnip lengthways into slices slightly thinner than a 10p coin. As you cut the slices, place them in a bowl of water. Repeat for the potato, celeriac, and beetroot, placing the slices of each vegetable into separate bowls of water. Set aside to soak for 20 minutes to remove the excess starch.

2 Pour 10 cm (4 inches) of sunflower oil into a deep-fat fryer or a large, heavy frying pan. Set over a moderately high heat and heat the oil to 190°C (375°F). Drain the vegetable slices and pat dry with kitchen paper or a clean tea towel. Carefully place a handful of parsnip slices in the hot oil and fry for about 3 minutes or until golden and crisp. Transfer to a wire rack lined with kitchen paper to drain. When the oil returns to 190°C (375°F), fry the remaining parsnip slices. Then deep-fry the potato slices, followed by the celeriac slices, and finally the beetroot slices in the same way, letting the oil return to 190°C (375°F) between each batch. The potato slices will take about 3 minutes; the celeriac and beetroot slices will take about 4 minutes and will crinkle slightly and not become crisp until they begin to cool.

3 Place the crisps in a bowl and season to taste with salt. Serve at once.

Serve with cocktails or a glass of berry-scented rosé from Provence.

1 large parsnip, peeled

1 baking potato, peeled

1 small celeriac, peeled and halved lengthways

1 large beetroot, peeled

Sunflower oil for deep-frying

Fine sea salt

Makes 6 servings

London gin

Gin, distilled from corn or barley and flavoured with juniper berries and other aromatics, has been associated with London since the Protestant William of Orange from Holland took over the throne from the Catholic King James II in 1688. Drinking Jenever, the early Dutch gin, became a symbol of Protestant patriotism. Parliament banned the import of wine and brandy from Catholic France and encouraged the wholesale distillation of gin. British distillers began to make huge quantities of the cheap and lethally strong drink, which was consumed by the poor and working class.

In the mid-eighteenth century, domestic gin production was reformed. Shortly thereafter, some of the great London gin distillers emerged: Philip Booth (1778) and Alexander Gordon (1786), both in Clerkenwell, Charles Tanqueray in Bloomsbury (1830), and James Burroughs in Chelsea (1863), known for Beefeater gin. They developed what became known as the London style of gin, using pure water from outlying villages and a continuous still to produce a light, dry gin that remains popular today.

SPICY THAI MEATBALLS WITH CHILLI AND LEMONGRASS SAUCE

When Thai restaurants first appeared in London in the 1970s, the combination of fragrant spices and Asian cooking methods immediately appealed to Londoners, who soon incorporated the cuisine into their own repertoire. Even supermarkets responded by starting to sell Thai curry pastes, fish sauce, kaffir lime leaves, coconut milk, fresh lemongrass, and other essential ingredients. As cooks experimented, they varied or simplified Thai dishes, and these meatballs, which are served on lettuce leaves with an aromatic dipping sauce, are a delicious example. The recipe can easily be doubled for a large party.

FOR THE SAUCE

1 lemongrass stalk

2 tablespoons sugar

½ teaspoon dried chilli flakes

4 tablespoons boiling water

2½ tablespoons white wine vinegar

FOR THE MEATBALLS

½ bunch fresh coriander, including stalks, finely chopped

2 spring onions, white and pale green parts only, finely chopped

1 clove garlic, finely chopped

Finely grated zest of 1 lemon

Finely ground black pepper

Pinch of freshly grated nutmeg

½ medium egg, lightly beaten

1½ teaspoons Thai fish sauce

175 g (6 oz) minced pork

Plain flour for coating

3 tablespoons sunflower oil

16 small, soft round lettuce leaves

Makes 6–8 servings

1 To make the sauce, trim off the upper leafy part of the lemongrass stalk and the tough end of the bulb. Remove the tough outer layer of the stalk. Finely slice the stalk and place in a small bowl with the sugar and chilli flakes. Add the boiling water and stir until the sugar has dissolved. Stir in the vinegar. Pour this sauce into a small bowl and set on a serving platter large enough to hold the lettuce leaves in a single layer.

2 To make the meatballs, combine the coriander, spring onions, garlic, lemon zest, a good grinding of black pepper, the nutmeg, egg, and fish sauce in a food processor. Pulse 4 or 5 times until puréed. Add the pork and pulse 2 or 3 times in short bursts until the mixture is well mixed. Do not overprocess the mixture, or it will have a gummy texture.

3 Place a generous amount of flour on a plate. Flour your hands, then pick up a walnut-sized piece of the pork mixture, dust it with flour, and lightly shape into a ball. Set aside on a clean plate. Repeat to make a total of 16 balls.

4 Preheat the oven to 200°C (400°F). In a non-stick frying pan over a moderately low heat, heat the oil. When the oil is hot but not smoking, gently add the meatballs and cook, turning as needed, for about 4 minutes or until lightly browned all over. Transfer to a plate lined with kitchen paper to drain. (The meatballs can be prepared to this point up to 24 hours ahead and kept in the fridge.)

5 Place the meatballs on a baking tray, cover with foil, and bake for about 20 minutes or until cooked through and piping hot. Arrange the lettuce leaves on the serving platter. Place a meatball on each lettuce leaf and serve with the sauce.

Serve with a light Thai beer such as Singha or a white wine such as an Austrian Grüner Veltliner or a dry German Riesling.

STILTON AND LEEK TART

Stilton cheese became famous in 1740 when Frances Paulet supplied Cooper Thornhill, owner of Bell Inn at Stilton, with her large rounds of nutty-tasting, blue-veined cow's milk cheese. The inn was a day's journey by coach from London on the Great North Road, and soon Thornhill was sending coach-loads of her excellent cheese to the capital. Stilton, still made in Nottinghamshire, Leicestershire, and Derbyshire, remains a favourite cheese. At Christmas, London cheesemongers display towering piles of mature truckles. Customers buy them to eat over the holidays, adding leftovers to soups, salads, and tarts.

1 To make the pastry, combine the flour and salt in a medium bowl. Rub in the butter until the mixture forms coarse crumbs. Alternatively, place the flour and salt in a food processor, add the butter, and pulse 4 or 5 times until the mixture forms coarse crumbs; transfer to a bowl. Using a fork, stir in enough of the cold water to form a rough dough. Turn the dough out on to a lightly floured work surface and lightly knead for about 30 seconds, just until smooth. Shape the dough into a disc 2 cm (¾ inch) thick, wrap tightly in cling film, and chill for at least 30 minutes or overnight.

2 On a lightly floured work surface, roll out the pastry dough into an evenly thick round about 25 cm (10 inches) in diameter, or large enough to line the bottom and sides of a 23 cm (9 inch) flan tin with a lift-out base. Drape the dough over the rolling pin and ease into the flan tin, pressing it into place. If there is an overhang, roll the rolling pin across the rim of the tin to cut it off. Prick the pastry case with a fork in several places, line with baking parchment, and fill with dried beans. Chill for 30 minutes.

3 Preheat the oven to 200°C (400°F). Bake the pastry case blind for about 15 minutes or until the pastry looks dry but is not coloured. Carefully remove the paper and beans. Set the pastry case aside. Reduce the oven temperature to 180°C (350°F).

4 To make the filling, cut each leek lengthways in half and rinse thoroughly. Trim away the dark green leaves. Thinly slice the white and pale green parts of the leeks and drain thoroughly. In a frying pan over a moderate heat, warm the sunflower oil. Add the leeks and cook, stirring occasionally, for about 4 minutes or until wilted. Transfer to a small bowl.

5 Place the cheese, whole egg, and egg yolk in a food processor and process until smooth. Transfer to a bowl and stir in the cream. Add the leeks and season with salt and pepper. Pour into the pastry case. Bake for about 25 minutes or until the filling is golden brown and just set. Serve the tart warm or at room temperature, cut into wedges.

Serve with a cassis-scented, medium-bodied red Bordeaux such as Pauillac.

FOR THE PASTRY

210 g (7½ oz) plain flour

Fine sea salt

115 g (4 oz) cold unsalted butter, diced

3–4 tablespoons cold water

FOR THE FILLING

5 small leeks

3 tablespoons sunflower oil

85 g (3 oz) Stilton cheese, or other strong blue cheese

1 medium egg, plus 1 medium egg yolk

120 ml (4 fl oz) double cream

Fine sea salt and freshly ground pepper

Makes 6 servings

PEA AND POTATO SAMOSAS

Golden, flaky samosas, piled on deli counters across London, tempt shoppers into indulging in a delicious spicy snack. The fillings vary but are generally either minced lamb and peas or diced potato and peas. At Indian restaurants, samosas are served as a starter, usually accompanied by a mildly spiced mint, coriander, or tamarind relish or mango chutney. They are easy to make at home and can be served piping hot as a snack, or for tea along with traditional Indian sweets. Amchoor powder, made from ground dried green mangoes, has a fruity, sour taste. It can be found at Asian supermarkets.

FOR THE FILLING

250 g (9 oz) new potatoes

2 tablespoons coarsely chopped fresh coriander

1½ tablespoons sunflower oil

½ small onion, finely diced

1 small fresh green chilli, or to taste, finely chopped

½ teaspoon peeled and finely chopped fresh ginger

½ teaspoon cumin seeds

75 g (2½ oz) fresh or frozen peas

2 teaspoons amchoor powder or fresh lemon juice (see above)

½ teaspoon garam masala

Fine sea salt

FOR THE PASTRY

140 g (5 oz) plain flour

¼ teaspoon fine sea salt

15 g (½ oz) unsalted butter, melted

75 g (2½ oz) plain yoghurt

Sunflower oil for deep-frying

Makes 4–6 servings

1 To make the filling, place the unpeeled potatoes in a medium saucepan with water to cover generously. Bring to the boil over a moderately high heat and cook for about 25 minutes or until tender. Drain. When the potatoes are cool enough to handle, peel and cut into 5 mm (¼ inch) cubes. Combine the potatoes and coriander in a bowl and set aside.

2 In a small saucepan over a moderately low heat, warm the sunflower oil. Add the onion, chilli, ginger, and cumin seeds and cook, stirring from time to time, for about 15 minutes or until the onion is soft and golden. Stir in the peas and 3 tablespoons water. Increase the heat to moderate, cover the saucepan, and simmer, stirring occasionally, for about 8 minutes or until the peas are tender. Uncover and continue to cook until any excess moisture has evaporated. Stir in the amchoor powder and garam masala. Add this mixture to the potatoes and stir gently to combine. Season to taste with salt and set aside to cool while you make the pastry.

3 To make the pastry, sift the flour and salt into a bowl. In a small bowl, stir together the melted butter and 2 tablespoons warm water. Add to the flour and stir to combine. Stir in 60 g (2 oz) of the yoghurt. Turn out on to a lightly floured work surface and knead for about 5 minutes or until stiff but pliable. Divide the pastry dough into 6 equal pieces.

4 Work with one piece of dough at a time. Roll it in the palm of your hand to form a round ball, dust with flour, and place on the work surface. Roll out into a thin disc about 15 cm (6 inches) in diameter. Cut the disc in half to make 2 half-moons and brush the edges with some of the remaining yoghurt. Place a spoonful of filling on one half of each half-moon. Fold the pastry over the filling to form a triangle. Pinch the edges to seal. Repeat to make a total of 12 samosas.

5 Pour 10 cm (4 inches) of sunflower oil into a deep-fat fryer or a large, heavy frying pan. Set over a moderately high heat and heat the oil to 190°C (375°F). Working in batches to avoid crowding the pan, carefully add a single layer of samosas and fry for about 4 minutes or until golden brown. Transfer to kitchen paper to drain. When the oil returns to 190°C (375°F), fry the remaining samosas.

6 Serve the samosas hot or warm with a relish or chutney (see above).

Serve with a light Indian beer such as Kingfisher or a spicy, full-bodied white wine such as Gewürztraminer.

MEDITERRANEAN MEZZE

Late into the night, particularly during the warm summer months, Londoners can imagine they are in the Middle East by strolling up and down the Marble Arch end of Edgware Road. The busy thoroughfare is lined with Middle Eastern juice bars, restaurants, and cafés. Friends gather to enjoy the evening air, watch the world go by, and share mezze – small dishes of tabbouleh, houmous, falafel, and walnut-stuffed aubergine, along with crisp fresh vegetables and freshly baked pitta bread – before moving on to kebabs or delicately spiced Iranian, Lebanese, or Egyptian stews.

1 To make the houmous, drain the chickpeas and place in a medium saucepan. Add fresh water to cover and bring to the boil over a high heat. Boil for 10 minutes, then reduce the heat, add the bicarbonate of soda, and cook for about 50 minutes or until the chickpeas are meltingly soft.

2 Meanwhile, make the tabbouleh. Place the bulgur wheat in a bowl with boiling water to cover and soak for 15 minutes. Drain, rinse, and squeeze dry. Thinly slice the 3 spring onions, using the white and pale green parts only. In a large bowl, combine the spring onions, bulgur wheat, olive oil, the juice of 1 lemon, the tomatoes, and the parsley. Season to taste with salt and pepper. Transfer to a serving bowl and set aside.

3 When the chickpeas are cooked, drain them, reserving the cooking water. In a food processor, purée the chickpeas and garlic until smooth. Add the juice of 2 lemons, the tahini, 4 tablespoons of the cooking water, and salt to taste. Pulse once or twice and check the consistency. If necessary, add more

cooking water to yield a soft, creamy paste. The houmous will thicken as it cools. Taste and adjust the seasoning. Transfer to a serving bowl, drizzle with olive oil, and sprinkle with the paprika. Set aside.

4 Peel the carrots and cucumber. Trim the ends of the carrots, then cut into sticks. Cut the cucumber in half lengthways and scoop out the seeds, then cut into sticks. Trim the bunch of spring onions, removing only the dark tops. Trim the radishes, leaving 5 mm (¼ inch) of the stalk intact.

5 Preheat the grill. Arrange the carrots, cucumber, spring onions, and radishes on a serving plate. Put the olives in a small bowl. Place the pitta breads on a baking sheet and toast under the grill for 1–2 minutes on each side or until hot and slightly crisp.

6 Cut the pitta breads into wedges and serve with the tabbouleh, houmous, vegetables, and olives.

Serve with a crisp Greek white wine from Santorini or an earthy red wine from Greece's Nemea region.

175 g (6 oz) dried chickpeas, soaked overnight in water to cover

½ teaspoon bicarbonate of soda

115 g (4 oz) bulgur wheat

3 spring onions, plus 1 bunch to serve

6 tablespoons extra virgin olive oil, plus more to drizzle

Juice of 3 lemons, or to taste

250 g (9 oz) tomatoes, skinned and finely chopped (see page 187)

60 g (2 oz) fresh flat-leaf parsley leaves, finely chopped

Fine sea salt and pepper

1 clove garlic, crushed

3 tablespoons tahini

½ teaspoon paprika

3 carrots

1 small cucumber

1 bunch small radishes

Handful of oil-cured green or black olives

6 pitta breads

Makes 6 servings

SOUPS AND SALADS

A fresh seasonal salad and a cup of classic watercress soup can be the

foundation for an impromptu picnic lunch in one of London's many parks.

Soups and salads form an integral part of the London diet, served for lunch or dinner, as a starter or as a main course, depending on how hearty they are. In the summer, spicy crab salad with avocado and refreshing cucumber soup make use of fresh vegetables and seafood from London's farmers' markets. Spanish-inspired chickpea, chorizo, and roast pepper salad is substantial enough for a light lunch, and rocket salad with quince cheese and thin slices of Parma ham stars on many smart restaurant menus. In the rainy winter months, nothing is more warming than a steaming bowl of pea soup.

CHICKPEA, TOMATO, AND CHORIZO SALAD

On Saturday mornings, London foodies head to Borough Market with its countless food stalls. The scent of chorizo sausages barbecuing over charcoal fills the air, and shoppers cannot resist eating a crusty sandwich filled with hot chorizo as they push through the crowds. The chorizo is sold by Brindisa, a small company that imports such Spanish delicacies as salted anchovies and paprika. Brindisa's products have transformed the city's menus, leading to widespread experimentation with Spanish ingredients, as in this salad.

1 To make the vinaigrette, in a large bowl whisk together the olive oil, vinegar, and garlic. Season to taste with salt and black pepper. Set aside.

2 Preheat the grill. Place the red sweet pepper quarters skin side up in the grill pan and grill for about 5 minutes or until the skin blisters and blackens. Transfer to a small bowl and cover with cling film.

3 When the sweet pepper quarters are cool enough to handle, peel off the skin. Cut the flesh into large dice. Add to the vinaigrette together with the tomatoes, onion, chickpeas, and parsley. Season to taste with cayenne, salt, and black pepper.

4 In a large frying pan over a moderate heat, warm the olive oil. Add the chorizo pieces and fry for 2–3 minutes on each side or until crisp. Transfer to kitchen paper to drain.

5 Add the chorizo to the salad and toss to combine. Taste and adjust the seasoning. Sprinkle with parsley and serve. The salad can be prepared up to 4 hours in advance and kept in the fridge. Bring to room temperature about 20 minutes before serving.

Serve with a spicy, medium-bodied Spanish red wine such as Rioja Crianza.

FOR THE VINAIGRETTE

6 tablespoons extra virgin olive oil

2 tablespoons red wine vinegar

1 clove garlic, finely chopped

Fine sea salt and freshly ground black pepper

2 red sweet peppers, quartered and seeded

500 g (1 lb 2 oz) tomatoes, skinned and diced (see page 187)

1 small red onion, diced

2 cans (400 g each) chickpeas, drained and rinsed

30 g (1 oz) fresh flat-leaf parsley leaves, coarsely chopped, plus more to garnish

Pinch of cayenne pepper, or to taste

Fine sea salt and freshly ground black pepper

1 tablespoon olive oil

250 g (9 oz) Spanish chorizo sausage, cut into half-moons

Makes 4 servings

Butchers

Every Saturday morning, a queue spills out from C Lidgate, the butcher shop in Holland Park Avenue. Inside, butchers frantically work to fill customers' orders – weighing home-made sausages, trimming joints of Aberdeen Angus beef, and cutting chops of Gloucester Old Spot pork. During winter months, Lidgate sells plump geese and game such as grouse and pheasant, and even offers a plucking and hanging service for Londoners who have returned from a weekend shoot.

In recent years, London butchers have developed a fashionable niche market for organic meat and specific breeds bought directly from farms. Lidgate, for example, buys organic beef and pork from Highgrove, Prince Charles's estate in Wiltshire. Some farmers have even opted to sell their meat directly to the public at London farmers' markets. The Ginger Pig, for example, was so successful in Borough Market selling meat from its Yorkshire farm that it opened a butcher shop in Marylebone. There customers can buy Ginger Pig bacon, made from dapper Berkshire or long-flanked Tamworth pigs, or order meltingly tender Swaledale lamb, a hardy hill breed.

SPICY CRAB, AVOCADO, AND WATERCRESS SALAD

In the 1970s, nearly every London bistro served an avocado and crab or prawn cocktail. The seafood was bathed in a lightly spiced tomato mayonnaise and piled into an avocado half placed on a bed of lettuce. Chefs gradually started to experiment with this iconic dish, and today you can order a superb classic crab salad seasoned and prepared at your table, as at Cecconi's in Mayfair. Or try the light, spicy version here, where the crab is dressed in a modest amount of mayonnaise and spiked with fresh lime juice, mint, and chillies. Rather than cook whole crabs, buy freshly cooked white crabmeat.

FOR THE CRAB SALAD

500 g (1 lb 2 oz) fresh white crabmeat

1 or 2 fresh red or green Thai chillies, finely diced

Finely grated zest of 2 limes

Juice of 1 lime

2 tablespoons coarsely chopped fresh mint

2 tablespoons mayonnaise

Fine sea salt

FOR THE DRESSING

6 tablespoons extra virgin olive oil

2 tablespoons fresh lime juice

Fine sea salt and freshly ground pepper

1 small red onion

2 hearts of cos lettuce, torn into pieces, or Little Gems, leaves separated

2 bunches watercress, trimmed into sprigs

3 avocados

Makes 6 servings

1 To make the crab salad, place the crabmeat in a medium bowl. Pick over the crabmeat to make sure that all pieces of shell have been removed. Using kitchen paper, gently pat the crabmeat dry. Add the chillies, lime zest and juice, mint, and mayonnaise and stir gently to combine. Season to taste with salt. Cover and keep in the fridge until serving.

2 To make the dressing, in a small bowl whisk together the olive oil and lime juice. Season to taste with salt and pepper.

3 Halve the onion lengthways, peel, and slice thinly. Set aside one-quarter of the onion to garnish. In a large bowl, combine the remaining onion with the lettuce and watercress. Drizzle over the dressing and toss gently together.

4 Halve each avocado and remove the stone. Peel each avocado half or, using a large metal spoon, carefully scoop out the flesh from each avocado half in one piece; discard the peel.

5 Divide the greens and onion among 6 individual plates. Top each with an avocado half. Spoon the crabmeat mixture on to each avocado half, garnish with the reserved onion, and serve.

Serve with a rich white Burgundy such as Meursault or a Tuscan Chardonnay.

WATERCRESS SOUP

For centuries bunches of watercress have been hawked on London's streets to be eaten by residents as a cure-all for winter ailments. Only in the last seventy years have greengrocers and markets sold watercress. Apart from being a favourite salad ingredient, the peppery green leaves are also good in creamy soups, and restaurants ranging from the Michelin-starred Orrery to the casual No 6 George Street serve it all summer. Hot watercress soup is often topped with crisp croutons, while cold soup is given a swirl of cream.

1 In a large saucepan over a moderate heat, warm the olive oil. Add the onion and cook, stirring occasionally, for about 5 minutes or until soft. Stir in the potatoes and cook for 2 minutes. Add the leeks, increase the heat to moderately high, and cook, stirring occasionally, for about 4 minutes or until the leeks begin to soften and wilt. Add the chicken stock and season with salt and pepper. Bring to the boil, then reduce the heat and simmer, uncovered, for about 25 minutes or until the vegetables are very soft.

2 Strip the watercress leaves from the stalks. Add the leaves to the saucepan and cook for about 3 minutes or just until they are soft enough to purée. The longer the watercress leaves cook, the more their rich green colour will fade.

3 Purée the soup in the pan with a hand-held blender, or transfer to a food processor and purée. Stir in the cream. Taste and adjust the seasoning.

4 If serving the soup hot, gently reheat it. To serve the soup cold, transfer to a serving bowl, cover, and chill for about 4 hours.

Serve with a lemony, crisp white wine such as Chablis.

4 tablespoons olive oil

1 onion, coarsely diced

2 large new potatoes, peeled and diced

500 g (1 lb 2 oz) leeks, white and pale green parts only, thinly sliced

1 litre (1¾ pints) home-made chicken stock or water

Fine sea salt and freshly ground pepper

2 bunches watercress

250 ml (8 fl oz) double cream

Makes 4 servings

English asparagus

Beginning early in May, bundles of English asparagus appear in markets and greengrocers all over London. Street vendors bellow out offers of "two for the price of one" for bunches of pencil-thin sprue. Restaurants offer an array of exquisite dishes – puréed asparagus soup or simple salads with grilled spears. The season is brief, a mere six weeks, but it marks the beginning of summer for Londoners, who will find any excuse to eat a plateful of tender spears dipped in melted butter or vinaigrette. Naturally, they believe English asparagus is the finest in the world.

Farmers claim that the temperate British weather causes the plants to grow slowly, which allows them to develop a superb taste. Most of the London crop comes from the Fens, but in centuries past, asparagus – known as "sparrow grass" – was grown in kitchen gardens surrounding London and along the Thames estuary. In the seventeenth and eighteenth centuries, growers extended the season by making composted hotbeds. Today, imported asparagus is available year round, but none compares with the flavour of home-grown asparagus.

CHICORY, PEAR, FETA, AND WALNUT SALAD

Londoners love good, simple food – especially food with a provenance. To ensure that a salad like this one tastes superb, they will seek out barrel-cured Greek feta cheese and French wet walnuts from speciality shops such as La Fromagerie, and the sweetest, ripest local organic pears, such as Comice or Concord, from their farmers' market. This trend began in the 1980s with London chefs Sally Clarke of Clarke's and Rowley Leigh of Kensington Place, who listed on their menus some of their best sources of ingredients, whether a purveyor of greens or a seller of a particular breed of duck.

FOR THE VINAIGRETTE

6 tablespoons walnut oil

2 tablespoons white wine vinegar or Champagne vinegar

Fine sea salt and freshly ground pepper

FOR THE SALAD

4 heads chicory

4 tablespoons coarsely snipped fresh chives

115 g (4 oz) walnut halves

225 g (8 oz) feta cheese, crumbled into 1 cm (½ inch) pieces

4 small ripe pears such as Comice or Concord

Makes 4 servings

1 To make the vinaigrette, in a small bowl whisk together the walnut oil and vinegar. Season to taste with salt and pepper. Set aside.

2 To make the salad, separate the leaves of the chicory. In a large bowl, combine the chicory leaves, chives, walnuts, and feta cheese.

3 If you wish, peel the pears. Cut each pear lengthways into quarters and, using a small, sharp knife, remove the core. Cut each pear quarter lengthways into thin slices.

4 Add the pear slices to the salad, drizzle with the vinaigrette, and toss gently to combine. Taste and adjust the seasoning. Divide the salad among 4 individual plates and serve at once.

Serve with a buttery white Burgundy such as Meursault or an apple-scented Bourgogne Blanc.

CHILLED CUCUMBER SOUP

A bowl of cool, fresh-tasting cucumber soup is perfect for a hot summer day in London and is often served in restaurants and at home. Long, smooth-skinned cucumbers first became popular in London in the eighteenth century. They were grown under glass cloches in hotbeds in the thriving market gardens of Pimlico, Fulham, Chelsea, Kensington, and other surrounding rural villages, where farmers also specialised in rare and out-of-season fruits and vegetables such as melons and winter asparagus. This classic recipe has been updated with crème fraîche.

1 Combine the milk, onion, bay leaf, and peppercorns in a small saucepan. Set over a low heat and heat slowly until small bubbles form round the edge of the pan. Remove from the heat, cover, and leave to infuse for 30 minutes.

2 Peel the cucumbers. Halve each cucumber lengthways and scoop out the seeds with a teaspoon. Set aside half of one cucumber for the garnish. Cut the remaining cucumber halves across into thick slices. In a large saucepan over a moderately low heat, melt the butter. Add the cucumber slices and sugar, season with salt and pepper, and cook, stirring occasionally, for 4–5 minutes or until the cucumber is soft. Stir in the flour and cook, stirring, for about 3 minutes or until the flour has thickened the liquid in the pan. Stir in the chicken stock, bring to the boil, and simmer for about 5 minutes.

3 Strain the milk mixture through a fine-mesh sieve into the saucepan and stir thoroughly. Simmer, uncovered, over a moderately low heat, stirring occasionally, for about 20 minutes or until thickened.

4 Purée the soup in the pan with a hand-held blender or transfer to a food processor and purée. Stir in the crème fraîche and season to taste with salt and pepper. Pour into a bowl, cover, and chill for about 4 hours.

5 To serve, finely dice the remaining cucumber half. Ladle the chilled soup into individual bowls and garnish with the diced cucumber and dill.

Serve with a refreshing, very dry white wine such as Muscadet or Sancerre.

300 ml (10 fl oz) whole milk

1 small onion, halved

1 fresh or dried bay leaf

2 black peppercorns

4 cucumbers

30 g (1 oz) unsalted butter

Pinch of caster sugar

Fine sea salt and freshly ground pepper

2 tablespoons plain flour

500 ml (16 fl oz) home-made chicken stock

175 g (6 oz) crème fraîche

1 teaspoon finely chopped fresh dill

Makes 4 servings

SORREL, LETTUCE, AND QUAIL'S EGG SALAD

Leafy green salads are popular among Londoners throughout the summer months. Fresh herbs, such as sorrel, mint, chervil, or tarragon, are often mixed in with choice salad leaves from farmers' markets. The salads are transformed by adding seasonal ingredients such as blanched green beans, asparagus tips, or broad beans, with lightly cooked quail's eggs or crisp bacon. Sorrel has a superb lemony acidity, which imbues the salad with a refreshing bite. If sorrel isn't available, you can use another favourite salad leaf such as mizuna. Similarly, one of the above vegetables can be substituted for the quail's eggs.

12 quail's eggs

2 bunches sorrel leaves, about 115 g (4 oz) total weight

2 soft round lettuces

3 fresh tarragon sprigs

6 spring onions, white parts only, thinly sliced

3 tablespoons extra virgin olive oil

1 tablespoon tarragon vinegar

1 teaspoon Dijon mustard

Fine sea salt and freshly ground pepper

Makes 4 servings

1 Put the quail's eggs in a small saucepan and cover with cold water. Bring to the boil over a high heat and boil for 2 minutes. Immediately plunge the eggs into cold water. Set aside to cool.

2 Strip away the stalks of the sorrel leaves by folding the sides of each leaf inwards and pulling the stalk towards the tip of the leaf. This will split the leaf in half. Tear the leaves into bite-sized pieces and place in a bowl. Remove the outer leaves from the lettuces until you reach the heart. Reserve the outer leaves for another use. Separate the leaves of the hearts, rinse, and dry. Add to the bowl with the sorrel leaves and toss to combine. Strip the leaves from the tarragon stalks and add to the salad together with the sliced spring onions.

3 Peel each quail's egg under cold running water, being sure to remove every speck of shell. Pat the eggs dry with a tea towel. Cut the eggs in half and add to the salad.

4 In a small bowl, whisk together the olive oil, vinegar, mustard, and salt and pepper to taste. Drizzle over the salad and toss gently to combine.

5 Arrange the salad on individual plates, dividing the quail's eggs evenly. Serve at once.

Serve with a smoky, dry white Sauvignon Blanc such as Pouilly-Fumé or Quincy.

JAPANESE PAN-FRIED SALMON SALAD

Over the past thirty years, Londoners have developed a taste for oriental cuisine, in particular, Japanese, Chinese, and Thai cooking. Initially, in the early 1980s, London cooks would haphazardly mix the different styles. A Japanese chicken teriyaki, for example, might be paired with Chinese pickled cucumbers. As Londoners' culinary knowledge expanded, they developed a fusion of ingredients, flavours, and cooking techniques to create a new style of modern British cooking. This contemporary salad exemplifies these influences.

1 To make the marinade, combine the soy sauce, honey, and ginger in a small saucepan. Set over a low heat and cook, stirring, until the honey is dissolved. Simmer for 1 minute, then remove from the heat. Add the lime zest. Leave to cool and infuse for 30 minutes. Whisk in the lime juice and sesame oil. Set aside.

2 In a bowl, combine the cucumber slices and ¼ teaspoon salt and set aside for 10 minutes. Stir in the sugar and vinegar. In a large bowl, combine the lettuce, rocket, and spring onions. Set aside.

3 Run your fingers gently over each salmon fillet to locate the pin bones and remove them with sturdy tweezers or needle-nosed pliers. In a non-stick frying pan over a high heat, warm the olive oil. Add the fillets skin side down and cook for about 5 minutes or until crisp. Turn and cook for another 5 minutes or until golden. Transfer to a dish and spoon over half of the marinade. Leave to cool.

4 Before serving, remove the skin from each fillet. Add the remaining marinade and the cucumber with any liquid to the salad leaves and toss to combine. Divide the salad among individual plates. Top each with a salmon fillet and serve at once.

Serve with Pilsner beer or a dry white wine such as Alsatian Riesling.

FOR THE MARINADE

4 tablespoons naturally brewed soy sauce (see page 187)

3 tablespoons clear honey

1 tablespoon peeled and finely grated fresh ginger

Finely grated zest of 2 limes

Juice of 1 lime

1 tablespoon toasted sesame oil

1 ridge cucumber, peeled and finely sliced

Fine sea salt

1 tablespoon caster sugar

1 tablespoon white wine vinegar

4 soft round lettuces, leaves separated

30 g (1 oz) rocket, trimmed

6 spring onions, white parts only, thinly sliced

4 salmon fillets, about 175 g (6 oz) each

3 tablespoons olive oil

Makes 4 servings

Oriental food shops

Despite London's vast size, the city is made up of village-like communities whose character is shaped in part by the different nationalities living there. With each influx of immigrants come new foods, shops, and restaurants. The Japanese, for example, have settled in North London along the Finchley Road, and there the shelves of small shops are stacked with mirin, bonito flakes, and dried seaweed, and fishmongers display glistening fresh fish.

Thai shops are scattered throughout London, but Richmond has particularly good ones, including Paya Thai and Talad Thai. Here, cooks can buy tiny pea aubergines, holy basil, tiny hot chillies, fresh galangal, and myriad dried spices for flavouring Thai curries and soups. Peckham and Dalston are known for Vietnamese shops, while Earl's Court has a Filipino shop selling a wide range of foods from purple yam jam to fresh banana leaves.

Most Londoners seeking exotic Chinese ingredients head for Chinatown in Soho, where well-stocked shops carry spices, dried mushrooms, wonton wrappers, Burmese pickles, and fresh lotus roots.

ROCKET SALAD WITH QUINCE CHEESE AND PARMA HAM

Every autumn, fragrant golden quinces are piled high in London's Middle Eastern food shops. Discerning customers bring them home to prepare syrups, puddings, and, best of all, quince cheese. Known also by its Spanish name, membrillo, *quince cheese has been made in England since the sixteenth century, when fruit pastes were served at the end of a meal with nuts and other sweetmeats. The cheese is enjoying renewed popularity with chefs such as Henry Harris of Racine and Samuel and Samantha Clark of Moro, who use it in starters such as this one, where it balances the salty ham and peppery rocket.*

FOR THE QUINCE CHEESE

1.35 kg (3 lb) quinces

Juice of 2 lemons

675–900 g (1½–2 lb) sugar, or as needed

1½ teaspoons sunflower oil

FOR THE SALAD

1 teaspoon fresh lemon juice

1½ tablespoons extra virgin olive oil

Fine sea salt and freshly ground pepper

140 g (5 oz) rocket, trimmed

250 g (9 oz) thinly sliced Parma ham

Makes 6 servings

1 To make the quince cheese, scrub the quinces well and then coarsely chop without peeling or coring them. Place in a large non-metallic saucepan with the lemon juice and enough water just to cover. Bring to the boil over a high heat, then reduce the heat to low, cover, and simmer for about 3 hours or until the quinces are very soft and a deep brownish pink.

2 Pass the quince mixture through a fine-mesh sieve set over a bowl, pressing on the solids with the back of a wooden spoon to extract as much purée as possible. Discard the solids. Measure the purée and allow 450 g (1 lb) sugar for every 500 g (1 lb 2 oz) of purée. Combine the purée and sugar in a large non-metallic saucepan, place over a low heat, and cook, stirring, until the sugar is dissolved. Increase the heat to high, bring to the boil, and cook, stirring constantly, until the mixture is so thick that the spoon leaves a clean line when drawn across the pan bottom and the purée is a uniformly dark, dusky pink. This will take about 25 minutes. As the hot purée thickens, it will splatter, so protect your hands and arms.

3 Meanwhile, lightly oil 3 sterilised 250 ml (8 fl oz) pots. Spoon the hot quince mixture into the pots to within 5 mm (¼ inch) of the tops. Allow to cool, then cover tightly with cling film and chill until set. (The pots of quince cheese can be kept in the fridge for up to 1 month.)

5 Turn out the quince cheese from one of the pots. Dip a sharp knife into very hot water and cut the cheese into slices 5 mm (¼ inch) thick. Then trim the slices into triangles or diamonds. Set aside.

6 To make the salad, in a large bowl, whisk together the lemon juice, olive oil, and salt and pepper to taste. Add the rocket and toss thoroughly. Arrange the Parma ham on 6 individual plates. Divide the rocket salad among the plates and scatter over the quince cheese triangles. Serve at once.

Serve with a creamy sherry from Spain such as Oloroso.

PEA SOUP

In the nineteenth century, soup made from dried peas was sold from street barrows around London to those looking for a quick, hot dinner. The peas were cooked into a very thick soup that was filling and that helped fend off the damp winter chill. The soup was known as London Particular after the famously dense, sulphurous smog that enveloped the city. To this day, very thick fog is called a pea souper. Old-fashioned winter pea soups such as this one are made with split peas, while lighter versions use fresh green peas. The former tend to be served in pubs or restaurants specialising in hearty fare.

1 Place the split peas in a large bowl, add cold water to cover generously, and leave to soak for at least 12 hours.

2 The next day, in a large saucepan over a low heat, warm the sunflower oil. Add the bacon and cook, stirring frequently, for about 3 minutes. Add the onion, garlic, carrot, and celery and cook, stirring from time to time, for about 10 minutes or until soft.

3 Drain the split peas and add to the pan together with the parsley leaves and 1.7 litres (3 pints) water. Bring to the boil over a high heat, then reduce the heat to low, partly cover, and simmer for about 2 hours or until the peas are meltingly soft. Halfway through the cooking time, add about 600 ml (1 pint) water to top up the cooking liquid.

4 Purée the soup in the pan with a hand-held blender or transfer to a food processor and purée. Strain the puréed soup through a coarse-mesh sieve into a clean saucepan. Gently reheat over a moderately low heat, stirring occasionally. Add a little water if the soup is too thick. Season to taste with salt and pepper.

5 Ladle the soup into warmed bowls, garnish with parsley leaves if you like, and serve at once.

Serve with a smoky white wine such as Pinot Gris.

200 g (7 oz) yellow or green split peas, picked over, rinsed, and drained

2 tablespoons sunflower oil

115 g (4 oz) streaky bacon, finely diced

1 onion, coarsely diced

1 clove garlic, coarsely chopped

1 carrot, peeled and coarsely diced

2 celery sticks, coarsely diced

Leaves of 1 fresh flat-leaf parsley sprig, plus more to garnish (optional)

Fine sea salt and freshly ground pepper

Makes 4 servings

MAIN COURSES

From savoury pies to classic roasts, contemporary seasonal dishes to kebabs and

curries, main dishes are defined by the delicious diversity of London cuisine.

Main dishes are characterised by their ability to stand alone as the well-balanced course of a meal. Hearty fish pie topped with fluffy mash, succulent roast beef with Yorkshire pudding, and steak, mushroom, and ale pie reflect an attachment to much-loved traditions. London's international character is evident in the long-standing popularity of Chinese, Indian, and Middle Eastern cuisines. As in other culinary meccas, chefs cook with the seasons, preparing lamb in spring and pheasant in autumn. Bacon and egg butties and bangers and mash fill the need for food that is both quick and satisfying.

FISH AND CHIPS

Londoners are fond of "going round to the chippie" to fetch piping-hot deep-fried fish and salty chips. The chips are usually seasoned with malt vinegar before being enclosed with the fish in paper. The wrapping was once newspaper, but that was banned years ago, despite claims that the printer's ink added a special flavour. The origin of fish and chips is uncertain. The selling of fried fish on London streets appeared in Charles Dickens's 1837 novel, "Oliver Twist", and by the 1850s, the foods were hawked on city streets. In 1860, Joseph Malin opened the first known fish-and-chip shop.

1 To make the chips, cut the potatoes lengthways into sticks about 5 mm (¼ inch) thick. Place in a bowl of cold water and set aside to soak for 20 minutes to remove the excess starch.

2 While the potatoes are soaking, begin to prepare the fish. Spread the flour on a plate and season with salt and pepper. Place the breadcrumbs on a separate plate. Put the egg into a shallow bowl, beat lightly, and season with salt and pepper. Dust each fish fillet with the seasoned flour, then dip into the beaten egg, letting the excess drip back into the bowl. Finally, dredge in the breadcrumbs, lightly pressing the crumbs on to all sides. Place the coated fillets in a single layer on a plate. Lightly cover with cling film and keep in the fridge until you are ready to cook.

3 Pour 10 cm (4 inches) of sunflower oil into a deep-fat fryer or a large, heavy frying pan. Set over a moderately high heat and heat the oil to 165°C (325°F). Drain the potatoes and pat dry with kitchen paper or a clean tea towel. Working in batches, carefully place the potatoes in the hot oil and fry for about 4 minutes or until crisp but not browned on the outside and tender but slightly firm on the inside. Do not crowd the pan or the oil will not be able to maintain the proper temperature. Using a slotted spoon, lift the potatoes from the hot oil, letting it drip back into the

pan, and transfer to a wire rack lined with kitchen paper to drain. When the oil returns to 165°C (325°F), fry the remaining potatoes. When the potatoes have cooled, they can be spread out on a baking sheet lined with kitchen paper and kept in the fridge for up to 4 hours until needed. Allow to return to room temperature before the second frying.

4 Shortly before you are ready to serve, heat the oil to 180°C (350°F). Again working in batches, place the potatoes in the hot oil and fry for 4–5 minutes or until golden and crisp. Transfer to kitchen paper to drain. Sprinkle with salt and toss gently.

5 To cook the fish, pour enough oil into a large non-stick frying pan to generously cover the bottom and set over a moderate heat. When the oil is hot, add the coated fillets and pan-fry for 4–6 minutes on each side or until golden brown. The timing will depend on the thickness of the fillets; do not let the breadcrumbs burn. Transfer the fillets to kitchen paper to drain.

6 Divide the fish and chips among 4 warmed individual plates. Garnish with the parsley sprigs and lemon quarters and serve at once.

Serve with a pint of pale ale or a full-bodied Chardonnay.

FOR THE CHIPS

4 large floury potatoes, peeled

Sunflower or corn oil for deep-frying

Fine sea salt

FOR THE FISH

2 tablespoons plain flour

Fine sea salt and freshly ground pepper

225 g (8 oz) dried white breadcrumbs

1 medium egg

4 cod or haddock fillets, about 140 g (5 oz) each, skin removed

Sunflower oil for pan-frying

4 fresh flat-leaf parsley sprigs

1 lemon, quartered

Makes 4 servings

BANGERS AND MASH WITH
RED ONION AND WINE GRAVY

Sausages roasted until mahogany brown and served with mash and a rich onion gravy are a favourite dish at local pubs and cafés and even at Michelin-starred restaurants. The British sausage became known as a banger around World War I, probably because it splutters as it fries. The sausages traditionally contain breadcrumbs mixed with minced pork, beef, or both. The bread gives them a softer consistency and a milder flavour than their continental counterparts. There are hundreds of recipes – often well-guarded secrets – the most famous being the unlinked spicy pork variety known as Cumberland.

1 kg (2¼ lb) good-quality pork sausages

1 tablespoon sunflower oil

FOR THE GRAVY

30 g (1 oz) unsalted butter

1 tablespoon olive oil

2 red onions, halved and finely sliced

1½ teaspoons plain flour

1 teaspoon red wine vinegar

250 ml (8 fl oz) red wine

250 ml (8 fl oz) home-made chicken or beef stock

Fine sea salt and freshly ground pepper

FOR THE MASH

1 kg (2¼ lb) floury potatoes, peeled and cut into large chunks

Fine sea salt and freshly ground pepper

6 tablespoons whole milk

30 g (1 oz) unsalted butter

Makes 4 servings

1 Preheat the oven to 200ºC (400°F). Put the sausages in a roasting tin, drizzle over the oil, and toss to coat, then spread them out in a single layer. Roast for about 30 minutes or until evenly coloured, turning them over after 15 minutes.

2 Meanwhile, make the gravy. In a wide, shallow saucepan over a moderately low heat, melt the butter with the olive oil. Add the onions and cook, stirring frequently, for about 4 minutes or until collapsed. Reduce the heat to low, cover the onions with roughly crumpled baking parchment, pressing it down on the onions, and cook for a further 20 minutes or until the onions are meltingly soft. Remove the paper and increase the heat to moderately low. Stir in the flour and cook for 2–3 minutes or until it is lightly coloured. Add the vinegar and cook, stirring, until it has evaporated. Stir in the red wine and stock, increase the heat, and bring to the boil. Simmer for about 10 minutes or until a luscious gravy forms. Season to taste with salt and pepper.

3 While the gravy is simmering, make the mash. Place the potato chunks in a saucepan with water to cover. Salt the water and bring to the boil over a moderate heat. Cook for 15–20 minutes or until the potatoes are tender when pierced with the tip of a knife. Drain in a colander, cover with a tea towel, and leave to dry for about 5 minutes. Meanwhile, in the same pan, combine the milk and butter and bring to the boil over a moderately high heat. Remove from the heat and keep warm. For the fluffiest texture, pass the cooked potatoes through a ricer or a food mill fitted with the medium disc. Alternatively, place in a bowl and mash with a potato masher. Add the hot milk mixture to the potatoes and beat until smooth. Season to taste with salt and pepper.

4 Divide the sausages and mash among warmed individual plates, spoon over the onion gravy, and serve at once.

Serve with a full-bodied amber beer, a Shiraz, or a red Beaujolais cru, such as Julienas or Morgon.

VENISON WITH RED WINE JUS AND ROASTED PARSNIPS

The arrival of autumn brings a change of emphasis in London restaurants. Gone from menus are summery fish dishes, to be replaced by heartier fare like venison with red wine jus, usually served with root vegetables such as parsnips, celeriac, or beetroot. Chefs can buy wild or farmed roe, fallow, or red deer. Most prefer the tender, mild farmed deer, which is available year round. Londoners traditionally eat venison with sweet, fruity accompaniments such as redcurrant jelly or pears poached in red wine with peppercorns.

1 Preheat the oven to 180°C (350°F). To make the jus, combine the shallot and wine in a saucepan and bring to the boil over a high heat. Cook for 20 minutes or until reduced to about 4 tablespoons. Add the stock, bring back to the boil, and cook for a further 40 minutes or until reduced to about 150 ml (5 fl oz). Stir in the Port. Reduce the heat to low and quickly whisk in the butter, a few pieces at a time. Remove from the heat and keep warm.

2 While the jus is reducing, place the parsnips on a baking tray in a single layer. Drizzle over the olive oil and toss to coat thoroughly. Season lightly with salt and pepper. Roast, stirring occasionally, for about 40 minutes or until soft and golden.

3 When the parsnips are nearly ready, in a non-stick frying pan over a high heat, warm the sunflower oil. When it is sizzling hot, season the venison steaks with salt and pepper and place them in the pan. Cook for about 3 minutes or until nicely browned. Turn and cook for about 2 minutes on the other side. The steaks will be medium rare; cook a little longer if you prefer them to be medium.

4 Place the steaks on individual plates. Spoon some red wine jus over each steak, top with the roasted parsnips, and serve at once.

Serve with a deep, red wine such as Bandol or a sturdy, full-bodied Cahors.

FOR THE RED WINE JUS

1 shallot, finely chopped

500 ml (16 fl oz) dry red wine

1 litre (1¾ pints) home-made chicken stock

3 tablespoons Port

60 g (2 oz) cold unsalted butter, diced

FOR THE ROASTED PARSNIPS

500 g (1 lb 2 oz) parsnips, trimmed, peeled, and cut lengthways into quarters

3 tablespoons olive oil

Fine sea salt and freshly ground pepper

3 tablespoons sunflower oil

4 venison steaks, about 200 g (7 oz) each and 1 cm (½ inch) thick, trimmed of excess fat

Fine sea salt and freshly ground pepper

Makes 4 servings

Wine merchants

Wine merchants have existed in London since Roman times. Over the centuries, they have stocked their cellars with fine English, French, German, Hungarian, Spanish, Italian, and New World wines. Compelled to buy wines that fit the nation's changing trade policies, merchants developed an extraordinary breadth of knowledge that has held them in good stead.

One example is Berry Bros & Rudd in St James's Street, SW1, London's oldest wine merchant. With its shop-front dating from the 1730s and its sloping floors, Berry Bros & Rudd might seem at first glance to be rather old-fashioned. It is, however, at the cutting edge of wine retailing. Behind the desks are computer screens, as much of the business comes from the company's innovative website. The staff are as adept at advising clients about building their own cellar as they are in recommending a wine for dinner. Their two-storey cellar houses a selection from the shop's stock of 2,500 wines along with racks of dusty bottles, including such gems as a bottle of 1858 Lafite Rothschild claret owned by the Berry and Rudd families.

SEARED DUCK BREASTS WITH POMEGRANATE MOLASSES AND SPINACH

In 1997, Samuel and Samantha Clark opened Moro, a popular restaurant in Exmouth Market, EC1, where they developed a menu that married Spanish, North African, and Middle Eastern cuisines with contemporary European cooking. It was a culinary style that has since influenced many other restaurants. This recipe, adapted from a dish served at Moro, uses sweet-and-sour pomegranate molasses to add an intriguing undercurrent of flavour to cinnamon-spiced duck breasts. Pomegranate molasses, widely used in Middle Eastern cooking, is the juice of the fruit reduced to a thick, dark syrup.

4 duck breasts, about 175 g (6 oz) each

Good pinch of ground cinnamon

Fine sea salt and freshly ground pepper

1 small clove garlic, finely chopped

3 tablespoons pomegranate molasses

1 teaspoon clear honey (optional)

FOR THE SPINACH

1 tablespoon olive oil

4 spring onions, white and pale green parts only, thinly sliced

500 g (1 lb 2 oz) baby spinach leaves, washed and dried

Fine sea salt and freshly ground pepper

Makes 4 servings

1 Trim any sinews from the duck breasts. Using a sharp knife, score the skin in a cross-hatch pattern, taking care not to cut into the meat. In a small bowl, stir together the cinnamon, 1 teaspoon salt, and a grinding of pepper. Rub the seasonings over both sides of the duck breasts. Place the breasts on a plate, cover with cling film, and chill for 2 hours.

2 Set a frying pan over a low heat and place the duck breasts in the pan, skin side down. Cook for about 3 minutes or until the fat begins to run. Increase the heat to moderate and cook for a further 5 minutes or until crisp and golden. Turn the breasts over and cook for another 5 minutes. Remove the breasts from the pan and set aside to rest in a warm place.

3 Pour off all but 1 tablespoon of the fat from the pan. Add the garlic and stir off the heat for about 45 seconds. When the pan has cooled slightly, return it to a low heat and add the pomegranate molasses and 6 tablespoons water. Cook, stirring occasionally, for about 1 minute or until reduced slightly. Season to taste with salt and pepper. The molasses is tart, so if you prefer a sweeter sauce, stir in the honey. Remove from the heat and set the pan aside.

4 To cook the spinach, in a wide saucepan over a high heat, warm the olive oil. Add the spring onions and cook, stirring occasionally, for 2–3 minutes or until softened. Add the spinach, a handful at a time, and stir until wilted. When all the spinach is in the pan and wilted, season to taste with salt and pepper.

5 To serve, reheat the sauce over a moderate heat. Slice each duck breast at an angle into 3 or 4 pieces and place on warmed individual plates. Add any juices from the duck breasts to the sauce and quickly bring to the boil, then pour over the breasts. Spoon the hot spinach beside the duck and serve.

Serve with a fruity red wine such as an Italian Primitivo or a smoky Syrah.

PAN-FRIED PHEASANT BREASTS WITH WILD MUSHROOM SAUCE

The Glorious Twelfth, the 12th of August, marks the beginning of the grouse season, and in London restaurants race to be the first to have grouse on the menu. On 1st October, the game season begins in earnest with the arrival of plump little partridges and young pheasants. They are so popular that supermarkets now sell them whole and in boneless breasts. In restaurants, pheasant breasts are often roasted and served either with a traditional bread sauce or a wild mushroom sauce like the one here. Accompany these pan-fried breasts with a creamy potato and celeriac mash.

1 To make the marinade, in a large bowl stir together 3 tablespoons of the olive oil, the lemon zest and juice, shallot, parsley sprigs, and a pinch of pepper. Wipe the pheasant breasts with damp kitchen paper and pick off any tiny feathers. Place in the bowl with the marinade and turn to coat. Cover with cling film and leave to marinate in the fridge for at least 1 hour or up to 3 hours.

2 To make the sauce, thickly slice or halve the mushrooms if they are large. In a wide saucepan over a low heat, warm 2 tablespoons of the olive oil. Add the shallots and garlic and cook for about 3 minutes or until soft. Increase the heat to moderate, add the mushrooms, and season to taste with salt and pepper. Cook for about 3 minutes or until the mushrooms have softened slightly. Pour in the vermouth and boil until reduced to a few tablespoons. Add the chicken stock, chopped parsley, and thyme

and boil for a further 5 minutes or until the liquid has reduced by half. Swirl in the butter. Taste and adjust the seasoning. Keep the mushroom sauce warm over a very low heat while you cook the pheasant breasts.

3 In a wide frying pan over a moderately high heat, warm the remaining 3 tablespoons olive oil. Remove the pheasant breasts from the marinade, pat dry, and season lightly with salt. Place in the pan and cook for 2–3 minutes on each side or until golden and the juices run clear when a breast is cut into with a sharp knife. Do not overcook or the pheasant breasts will be tough.

4 Place the pheasant breasts on warmed individual plates. Spoon over the mushroom sauce and serve immediately.

Serve with a rich, full-bodied aged red Burgundy or Châteauneuf-du-Pape.

120 ml (4 fl oz) olive oil

Finely grated zest of 1 lemon

2 tablespoons fresh lemon juice

1 shallot, thinly sliced

2 fresh flat-leaf parsley sprigs, bruised

Freshly ground pepper

4 skinned pheasant breasts, about 140 g (5 oz) each

300 g (10 oz) fresh wild mushrooms such as chanterelles and ceps, brushed clean and trimmed

2 shallots, finely chopped

1 clove garlic, finely chopped

Fine sea salt

120 ml (4 fl oz) dry vermouth, such as Chambery, or dry white wine

250 ml (8 fl oz) home-made chicken stock

4 tablespoons chopped fresh flat-leaf parsley

1 teaspoon chopped fresh thyme

30 g (1 oz) unsalted butter, diced

Makes 4 servings

STEAK, MUSHROOM, AND ALE PIE

Pies and pubs go together. Good gastropubs serve satisfying savoury pies, such as steak and mushroom or chicken and leek, often accompanied by potatoes and vegetables in season. Londoners have eaten pies since medieval times, when few dwellings had ovens. Consequently, many went to cookshops or public eating houses that sold pies and roast meats as well as ale and wine. This tradition continues today, although many cooks bake savoury pies at home. Rather than make your own puff pastry, you can use 675 g (1½ lb) of good-quality frozen puff pastry.

300 g (10 oz) plain flour, plus 5 tablespoons

Fine sea salt and freshly ground pepper

300 g (10 oz) cold unsalted butter

6 tablespoons sunflower oil, or as needed

1 kg (2¼ lb) braising steak, trimmed of fat and cut into 2.5 cm (1 inch) cubes

2 onions, peeled and sliced

2 large carrots, peeled and sliced

2 celery sticks, thinly sliced

1 clove garlic, finely diced

250 g (8 oz) button mushrooms, brushed clean and trimmed

2 teaspoons soft brown sugar

2 tablespoons white wine vinegar

250 ml (8 fl oz) light ale

3 strips lemon zest

3 sprigs fresh flat-leaf parsley

3 sprigs fresh thyme

2 cloves

1 bay leaf

1 egg, beaten

Makes 6 servings

1 To make the pastry, sift 300 g (10 oz) flour and a pinch of salt into a bowl. Rub in 30 g (1 oz) of the butter until the mixture forms fine crumbs. Stir in 120 ml (4 fl oz) cold water to form a smooth dough. Turn out on to a lightly floured work surface and knead until smooth. Shape the dough into a rectangle, wrap in cling film, and chill for at least 30 minutes.

2 Using a rolling pin, flatten the remaining butter into a rectangle 1 cm (½ inch) thick. On a lightly floured surface, roll the dough into a rectangle 3 times longer and 2.5 cm (1 inch) wider than the butter. Place the butter in the centre of the dough and fold the dough over the butter so it is enclosed. Using the rolling pin, press down on the edges to seal. Turn the dough over and, with a short side facing you, roll out until it returns to its original length. Fold the bottom third of the dough up and the top third down, as if folding a letter, then rotate the dough a quarter turn clockwise so that a fold is on your left (this is the first "turn"). Wrap the dough in cling film and chill for 30 minutes. Repeat to make 5 more turns, rotating the dough clockwise each time. If the dough becomes warm and starts to soften, chill before continuing. When completed, wrap the dough in cling film and chill for 1 hour.

3 In a saucepan over a moderate heat, warm 3 tablespoons of the oil. Place 3 tablespoons of the remaining flour on a plate and season with salt and pepper. Coat half of the beef cubes with seasoned flour, shaking off the excess, and add to the pan in one layer. Brown the cubes on all sides, then transfer to a bowl. Repeat with the remaining beef cubes.

4 Add the rest of the oil to the pan, reduce the heat to low, and add the onions, carrots, celery, and garlic. Cook, stirring occasionally, for 8–10 minutes or until soft. Increase the heat to moderate, stir in the mushrooms and brown sugar, and cook until lightly browned. Stir in the remaining 2 tablespoons flour and cook for 3–4 minutes. Add the vinegar and cook for 30 seconds, then add the ale, lemon zest, and 300 ml (10 fl oz) water. Return the beef to the pan. Tie up the parsley and thyme sprigs, cloves, and bay leaf in a square of muslin, and add to the pan. Bring to the boil, then reduce the heat to low, cover, and simmer for 1½ hours or until the meat is tender. Taste and adjust the seasoning. Set aside to cool for 1 hour.

5 Line a baking sheet with baking parchment. Have ready 6 individual pie dishes of 360 ml (12 fl oz) capacity. On a floured work surface, roll out the pastry into a rectangle 5 mm (¼ inch) thick. Cut out 6 rounds that are 5 mm (¼ inch) larger than the top of the dishes. Arrange the rounds on the baking sheet, prick with a fork, and chill for 30 minutes.

6 Preheat the oven to 200ºC (400°F). Remove the muslin bundle and lemon zest from the filling, then divide it among the 6 pie dishes. Brush the rim of each dish with beaten egg. Lay a pastry round on top and press the edges down with a fork to seal. Brush the pastry lids with beaten egg. Bake the pies for 15 minutes, then reduce the oven temperature to 180ºC (350°F) and bake for a further 25 minutes or until the pastry is golden brown. Serve the pies hot.

BACON AND EGG BUTTIES

Bacon and eggs have been regarded by the British as wholesome fare since the sixteenth century but were put into sandwiches only in the latter part of the nineteenth century, when sandwiches became popular. Londoners, always keen to adopt slang, like to refer to bacon sandwiches as "bacon sarnies" or "bacon butties". The best bacon and egg butties are made at home, but they can be bought from local cafés or sandwich bars throughout the city. They are the perfect all-day breakfast.

1 If using rolls or baps, slice them in half. Generously butter the rolls or bread slices and divide among 4 plates. Set aside.

2 Set 2 large frying pans over a moderately high heat and add 2 tablespoons sunflower oil to each pan. When the oil is sizzling hot, add half of the bacon rashers, in a single layer, to each pan and cook for about 2 minutes on each side or until they begin to colour and become crisp.

3 Stack the bacon rashers in each pan and push to one side. Reduce the heat to low and gently crack 2 eggs into each pan without breaking the yolks. Cook for 1 minute, then turn the eggs over and cook for a further 1–2 minutes or until the yolk is partly set but still somewhat soft, or until cooked to your taste.

4 Divide the bacon rashers among the plates, placing them on one of the buttered bread slices. Top with a fried egg and season to taste with salt and pepper. Cover with the remaining bread slices, buttered side down, and press firmly. Cut the sandwiches in half and serve straight away.

Serve with tea, coffee, or chilled Champagne.

4 good-quality soft white bread rolls or baps, or 8 thick slices cottage loaf or good-quality white bread

Softened unsalted butter as needed

4 tablespoons sunflower oil

500 g (1 lb 2 oz) smoked streaky bacon

4 medium eggs

Fine sea salt and freshly ground pepper

Makes 4 servings

London's classic cafés

Fifty years ago, a new form of café arrived in cosmopolitan Soho. In 1953, Gina Lollabrigida opened Moka in Frith Street, which served as a template for the hundreds of London cafés that followed. These new cafés, also called coffee bars, were dominated by a steaming espresso machine, the recent invention of Achille Gaggia.

The cafés were at the cutting edge of postwar culture and became hotbeds of creativity for the film, fashion, music, literary, and advertising worlds. Each café attracted a different crowd, but perhaps the most famous was the 2i's in Soho, a cellar frequented by musicians including Cliff Richard and Tommy Steele. By 1960, London had five hundred cafés, where young people hung out, drinking cappuccino ("frothy coffee") and eating early morning fry-ups (eggs, sausages, bacon, tomatoes, baked beans, and fried bread). Moka and the 2i's are long gone, but newer classics, such as E Pellicci in Bethnal Green Road, E1, and Bar Italia in Frith Street, W1, now fill the void. London cafés remain places where all classes of society sit side by side as they savour a Danish pastry or read the paper.

ROAST BEEF AND YORKSHIRE PUDDING

On Sunday mornings, the enticing aroma of roasting beef wafts down London streets. It conjures up the tempting taste of everyone's favourite Sunday lunch: roast beef and Yorkshire pudding baked in the hot dripping from the beef. First appearing in the eighteenth century, the dish is believed to have originated in the north of England. It is still a treat to eat roast beef at such venerable London establishments as Simpson's-in-the-Strand, favoured by Charles Dickens and William Gladstone, or the Grill Room in the Dorchester Hotel, patronized by Winston Churchill and Peter Sellers.

1 beef rib joint with 2 bones, about 2 kg (4½ lb)

1 tablespoon sunflower oil

Fine sea salt and freshly ground pepper

FOR THE YORKSHIRE PUDDINGS

140 g (5 oz) plain flour

¼ teaspoon fine sea salt

2 medium eggs, beaten

175 ml (6 fl oz) whole milk

FOR THE HORSERADISH SAUCE

3 tablespoons freshly grated horseradish

175 g (6 oz) crème fraîche

FOR THE GRAVY

2 tablespoons plain flour

120 ml (4 fl oz) dry white wine

400 ml (14 fl oz) home-made beef stock

Makes 6 servings

1 Preheat the oven to 165ºC (325ºF). Place a rack in a roasting tin just large enough to hold the joint of beef. Rub the meat all over with the sunflower oil and season with salt and pepper. Place fat side up on the rack and roast for about 1 hour and 40 minutes for medium-rare. A meat thermometer inserted into the thickest part away from the bone should register 52–54ºC (125–130ºF).

2 Meanwhile, to make the batter for the Yorkshire puddings, sift the flour and salt into a bowl. Make a well in the centre and gradually add the eggs, beating with a wooden spoon. Add 4 tablespoons of the milk and beat until smooth. Gradually beat in the remaining milk, then beat vigorously for a further 1 minute. Cover the bowl with cling film and set aside for 1 hour.

3 To make the horseradish sauce, in a small bowl stir together the horseradish, crème fraîche, and salt and pepper to taste. Set aside.

4 When the beef is cooked, remove it from the oven. Transfer to a platter, cover loosely with aluminium foil, and set aside to rest in a warm place. Increase the oven temperature to 220ºC (425ºF). Spoon ½ teaspoon of the beef dripping from the roasting tin into each of 4 large muffin tins. Place them in the oven to heat for about 3 minutes or until the fat is sizzling hot. Remove

from the oven and divide the pudding batter among the tins, then bake for 15–20 minutes or until the puddings are puffed up and have a golden crust.

5 While the puddings are baking, make the gravy. Pour off all but about 2 tablespoons of the dripping from the roasting tin and place it over a moderate heat. Using a wooden spoon, stir in the flour and cook until well blended with the dripping. Add the wine, bring to the boil, and deglaze the tin, stirring to remove any browned bits from the bottom. Continue to stir vigorously until the mixture thickens into a paste. Immediately stir in the stock. Bring to the boil and cook, stirring, for about 5 minutes or until slightly thickened. Season to taste, then strain the gravy through a fine-mesh sieve into a saucepan. Keep warm over a low heat until ready to serve.

6 Just before the puddings are ready, carve the beef and arrange on individual plates. Remove the puddings from the oven and, using the tip of a knife, lift from the tins, then add to the plates. Serve with the gravy and horseradish sauce.

Serve with a full-bodied, spicy red Bordeaux from Saint-Emilion.

OMELETTE ARNOLD BENNETT

This omelette, which makes an ideal after-theatre supper, was created in 1929 for the novelist Arnold Bennett while he was living at the Savoy Hotel, researching the backstairs life of a luxury hotel for his novel Imperial Palace. *According to legend, he requested the same dish each night from the Savoy Grill: a smoked haddock and cheese omelette. Today, the Savoy Grill offers a luxuriously rich version topped with a glaze of reduced fish stock, Noilly Prat vermouth, and cream. This recipe is simpler, but no less delicious.*

1 Preheat the grill. Cut the haddock or cod fillet in half and place the halves in a single layer in a wide saucepan. Add the parsley, peppercorns, bay leaf, and milk. Set over a moderate heat and heat until bubbles start to appear round the edge of the pan. Reduce the heat to low and simmer for 3–5 minutes or until the fish flakes when a knife is inserted into the thickest part. Using a slotted spoon, transfer the fish to a plate to cool. Discard the milk mixture.

2 When the fish is cool enough to handle, remove the skin. Break the flesh into rough flakes, discarding any small bones, and place in a small bowl. Stir in the cheese and season with pepper.

3 Set two 18 cm (7 inch) ovenproof omelette pans over a moderately high heat and add half of the butter to each pan. When the butter has melted, tilt the pans to spread the butter evenly. Pour half of the beaten eggs into each pan. Cook for about 1 minute, stirring with a wooden spatula, until the base is set but the top is still liquid. Quickly spoon the fish mixture over the eggs and drizzle the cream over the fish. Transfer to the grill and grill for about 6 minutes or until the omelettes are bubbling and flecked with brown.

4 Remove the pans from the grill and slide the omelettes on to warmed plates. Sprinkle with chives and serve at once.

Serve with a buttery Italian Chardonnay from Piedmont or a white Burgundy.

250 g (9 oz) smoked haddock or smoked cod fillet

1 fresh flat-leaf parsley sprig

3 black peppercorns

1 fresh bay leaf

500 ml (16 fl oz) whole milk

115 g (4 oz) Gruyère cheese, coarsely grated

Freshly ground pepper

30 g (1 oz) unsalted butter

4 medium eggs, lightly beaten with a pinch of fine sea salt

4 tablespoons double cream

Coarsely snipped fresh chives, to garnish

Makes 2 servings

London smoked fish

"London smoke" refers to a light, delicate style of smoked fish developed in the East End by Jewish immigrants. Fleeing their homes in eastern Europe from 1860 until 1905, they brought with them an expertise in curing fish, which they applied to two foods the British adored: haddock and salmon. Before this, both fish were always smoked in Scotland.

For many years, the East End was peppered with the chimneys of smokehouse brick kilns. With the arrival of inexpensive farmed Scottish salmon, small firms were unable to make a profit smoking the fish and gradually went out of business. H. Forman & Son, however, remained. Founded in 1905, the family-run smokehouse thrived by developing the upper end of the market. Their salmon, both wild and farmed, is cured in salt, then smoked over smouldering oak chips. To expand the business, H. Forman & Son incorporated another old East End firm, F & D Lewzey, which specialised in smoking haddock, herring, and sprats. The plump haddock fillets are brined, spiked with sugar, and smoked over oak and beech sawdust. H. Forman & Son fish is sold in the top London food halls.

SEARED SCALLOPS WITH TAGLIATELLE, BROAD BEANS, AND BACON

Freshly picked broad beans in their velvety pods first appear in farmers' markets throughout London in June. Londoners eagerly take them home, pod the beans, and cook them briefly, then toss them into salads, purée them in creamy soups seasoned with sage, or add them to light pasta sauces like the one here. Bacon, a traditional British partner for broad beans, enhances their sweetness. Pancetta, the Italian cured bacon, can be substituted. When buying broad beans, try to find young, small beans as they will be more tender. It is important that the sauce be ready at the same time as the pasta.

150 g (5½ oz) podded broad beans

Fine sea salt

250 g (9 oz) dried tagliatelle or fettuccine

120 ml (4 fl oz) extra virgin olive oil

500 g (1 lb 2 oz) scallops, cut into quarters

250 g (9 oz) back bacon, diced

12 spring onions, white and pale green parts only, thinly sliced

2 cloves garlic, finely chopped

Finely grated zest of 2 lemons

2 tablespoons fresh lemon juice

Freshly ground pepper

Makes 4 servings

1 Bring a small saucepan of water to the boil over a high heat. Add the beans and boil for 3–4 minutes or just until tender. Drain in a colander and refresh in cold water. If using large, older beans, pinch each bean to slip it from its skin. Discard the skins and set the beans aside.

2 Bring a large pan of water to the boil over a high heat. Salt the water, then add the pasta, stir, and cook according to packet directions until al dente.

3 While the pasta is cooking, in a frying pan over a high heat, warm 3 tablespoons of the olive oil. Add the scallops and sear for 1 minute on each side. Remove from the pan and set aside. Add another 3 tablespoons oil to the pan and reduce the heat to moderate. Add the bacon and cook, stirring frequently, for about 5 minutes or until it just begins to turn crisp. Stir in the spring onions and garlic and cook for a further 1 minute or until they begin to soften and

become fragrant. Add the broad beans, scallops, and lemon zest. Cook, stirring occasionally, for another minute or until heated through.

4 When the pasta is ready, drain and return to the pan. Add the remaining 2 tablespoons oil to the pasta and toss to coat. Add the lemon juice to the sauce and season with salt and pepper to taste. Add the sauce to the pasta. Toss gently to combine, then divide among warmed individual plates, and serve.

Serve with a full-bodied dry white wine such as an Italian Verdicchio.

FISH PIE

This pie is a classic example of what the British refer to as "nursery food" – sophisticated versions of childhood dishes for adults, who find the seafood filling in a luscious sauce, topped with creamy mash, very comforting indeed. Traditional fish pies primarily use fresh white-fleshed fish with prawns and other shellfish, but this version also includes smoked haddock or cod to add a distinctive and appealing depth of flavour. The pie can be topped with puff pastry (see page 136) rather than mash, if you prefer. Tiny, sweet petit pois are a favourite accompaniment to a fish pie.

1 To make the topping, place the potato chunks in a saucepan with cold water to cover generously and salt the water. Bring to the boil over a moderate heat and cook for about 20 minutes or until tender. Drain in a colander, cover with a tea towel, and leave to dry for about 5 minutes. For the fluffiest texture, pass the cooked potatoes through a ricer. Alternatively, place in a bowl and mash with a potato masher. Beat in the butter. Pour in the milk and beat until smooth. Season to taste with salt and pepper.

2 While the potatoes are cooking, make the filling. Combine the fresh fish fillets, milk, cream, peppercorns, parsley, and bay leaf in a wide pan. Set over a moderate heat and bring to a simmer. Cook for 5–8 minutes or until the fish will flake when a knife is inserted into the thickest part. The timing will depend on the thickness of the fillets. Using a slotted spoon, transfer the fillets to a shallow bowl. Immerse the smoked fish fillets in the milk mixture, bring to a simmer, and cook for about 3 minutes or until the fish flakes when a knife is inserted into the thickest part. Using the slotted spoon, transfer the fillets to the bowl. Strain the milk mixture and reserve. As the fish cools, add any liquid in the bowl to the strained milk mixture.

3 In a saucepan over a low heat, melt the butter. Using a wooden spoon, stir in the flour and cook, stirring constantly, for 2 minutes. Stir in the vermouth and cook until thick and smooth. Slowly add the strained milk mixture, stirring constantly, and cook for about 6 minutes or until a thick, smooth sauce forms. Reduce the heat to low and simmer, stirring frequently, for about 5 minutes. Remove the sauce from the heat, stir in the lemon juice, and season to taste with salt and pepper. Set aside.

4 Preheat the oven to 190°C (375°F). Break the cooked fish into large flakes, discarding any small bones, and place in a large bowl. Peel and devein the prawns. If they are large, cut into bite-sized pieces. Remove any tough, white muscle from the side of each scallop, then cut them in half. Add the scallops and prawns to the fish. Pour in the sauce and stir gently to combine. Divide the filling among 6 individual baking dishes or a 23 cm (9 inch) square baking dish about 7.5 cm (3 inches) deep. Top with the potato mixture, spreading it evenly to cover the filling. Using a fork, fluff the potatoes to create a textured surface.

5 Bake until the topping is golden and the filling is bubbling, about 30 minutes for individual pies and 50 minutes for a large pie. Serve hot.

Serve with a herby, minerally white Burgundy such as Puligny-Montrachet.

FOR THE TOPPING

1 kg (2¼ lb) floury potatoes, peeled and cut into large chunks

Fine sea salt and freshly ground pepper

85 g (3 oz) unsalted butter, at room temperature

6 tablespoons whole milk

FOR THE FILLING

250 g (9 oz) fresh haddock or cod fillets, skin removed

250 ml (8 fl oz) whole milk

150 ml (5 fl oz) double cream

5 black peppercorns

3 fresh flat-leaf parsley sprigs

1 bay leaf

675 g (1½ lb) smoked haddock or cod fillets, skin removed

15 g (½ oz) unsalted butter

2 tablespoons plain flour

150 ml (5 fl oz) dry vermouth such as Noilly Prat

2 tablespoons fresh lemon juice

250 g (9 oz) raw prawns

250 g (9 oz) raw scallops

Makes 6 servings

STEAMED SEA BASS WITH GINGER AND BLACK BEANS

Chinese immigrants have lived and worked around the docks in London's Limehouse since the 1850s. After the heavy bombing during World War II, they moved to Soho, where they were joined by farmers from Hong Kong. By the 1960s, Soho's Chinatown was thriving and became famous for its restaurants serving Cantonese food. The influence of Chinese cuisine has never abated. This recipe is an adaptation of a dish served at the Oriental Restaurant, which opened in 1990 at the Dorchester Hotel in Mayfair. Accompany the fish with steamed rice and stir-fried baby pak choi or Chinese greens.

1 tablespoon dried mandarin peel (see page 186), or 5 strips dried tangerine peel, about 1 cm (½ inch) wide and 4 cm (1½ inches) long

1 tablespoon sunflower oil

2 cloves garlic, peeled

2 tablespoons fermented black beans, chopped (see page 186)

2 tablespoons oyster sauce

1 tablespoon Chinese rice wine (see page 185) or dry sherry

1 tablespoon toasted sesame oil

¼ teaspoon corn oil

1 tablespoon caster sugar

1½ teaspoons cornflour mixed with 3 tablespoons cold water

2 spring onions, white and pale green parts only, thinly sliced on the diagonal

1 small, fresh red or green chilli, thinly sliced

1 cm (½ inch) piece fresh ginger, peeled and finely grated

4 sea bass fillets, about 175–225 g (6–8 oz) each

Makes 4 servings

1 Place the mandarin peel in a small bowl, add cold water to cover, and leave to soak for about 1 hour or until soft. Drain and finely chop. If using dried tangerine strips, grind them to a coarse powder in a mortar and pestle or an electric spice grinder. Set aside.

2 In a small saucepan over a low heat, warm the sunflower oil. Add the garlic and cook for 1 minute; do not allow it to brown. Add the black beans and cook gently for about 2 minutes or until they are infused with the garlic oil. Remove from the heat and stir in the oyster sauce, rice wine, sesame oil, corn oil, sugar, and mandarin peel or tangerine peel. Bring to the boil, then reduce the heat to low and simmer very gently for about 10 minutes. Add the cornflour mixture, stir vigorously, and simmer for a further 2 minutes or until thickened. Pour the sauce into a bowl and leave to cool for about 30 minutes.

3 Stir the spring onions, chilli, and ginger into the sauce. Add the fish fillets and leave to marinate for 10 minutes. Place 2 of the fillets, side by side, on a sheet of aluminium foil. Spoon half of the sauce over the fillets and turn to coat in the sauce, then place them skin side down. Seal the foil tightly. Repeat with the 2 remaining fillets. Place the foil parcels in separate compartments of a bamboo steamer or other steamer rack and cover tightly.

4 Pour water into a wok or other pan and bring to the boil. Place the steamer over the wok and cook for about 12 minutes or until the fish is opaque throughout and will flake when tested with a knife. Carefully remove the parcels from the steamer. Gently unwrap them and divide the fillets and sauce among warmed plates. Serve at once.

Serve with a rose-scented white wine such as an Alsatian Gewürztraminer.

CHICKEN TIKKA MASALA

Indian food is so loved by the British that it is now regarded as an essential part of the national diet. The taste for curried dishes was developed in the eighteenth century, but it was not until the 1960s that Indian restaurants began to influence British eating habits. Soon, every neighbourhood had an Indian restaurant where locals could enjoy a meal or order their favourite takeaway. One of the most popular dishes, a uniquely British invention, is chicken tikka masala, succulent cubes of chicken breast bathed in a sweet, spicy sauce.

1 In a large bowl, stir together the yoghurt, lime juice, 2 teaspoons ginger, 1 teaspoon each of cumin and garam masala, and the paprika. Trim excess fat from the chicken and cut into 2.5 cm (1 inch) cubes. Add to the bowl and stir, then cover and marinate in the fridge for at least 1 hour or up to 7 hours.

2 Preheat the grill to high. Remove the chicken from the marinade, shaking off the excess, and place on a plate. Season with salt and drizzle over 2 tablespoons sunflower oil; toss to coat. Arrange the chicken in a single layer in a foil-lined baking tray and grill for about 3 minutes on each side or until browned. Alternatively, heat a ridged cast-iron grill pan over a moderately high heat, add the chicken in a single layer, and chargrill for about 3 minutes on each side. Set aside.

3 To make the masala sauce, in a saucepan over a moderate heat, warm the remaining sunflower oil. Add the onion, remaining ginger, and the garlic and cook, stirring frequently, for 4–5 minutes or until the onion is soft. Add the cardamom, coriander, turmeric, ground chilli, and remaining cumin and cook, stirring, for 2 minutes. Add the tomatoes and cook, stirring frequently, for 5–8 minutes or until the oil separates out from the tomato mixture. Add the chilli, cream, and 120 ml (4 fl oz) water and bring to the boil. Reduce the heat to low and simmer for 8–10 minutes or until a creamy sauce is formed. Stir in the cooked chicken and remaining garam masala, season to taste with salt, and simmer for another 8–10 minutes or until the chicken is heated through. Stir in the lemon juice. Serve hot, with warm naan breads.

60 g (2 oz) Greek yoghurt

Juice of 1½ limes

3 teaspoons peeled and finely chopped fresh ginger

2 teaspoons ground cumin

1¼ teaspoons garam masala

2 teaspoons paprika

4 skinless, boneless chicken breasts, about 125 g (4½ oz) each

Fine sea salt

5 tablespoons sunflower oil

1 small onion, finely diced

1 clove garlic, finely chopped

5 green cardamom pods

1 teaspoon ground coriander

½ teaspoon *each* ground turmeric and ground chilli

500 g (1 lb 2 oz) tomatoes, skinned, seeded, and diced (see page 187)

1 fresh green chilli, thinly sliced

120 ml (4 fl oz) double cream

Juice of ½ lemon

Warm naan breads

Makes 4 servings

Indian food shops

When shoppers step into grocers such as Nita Cash & Carry in Wembley, the scent of incense sticks mingling with the aroma of spices and sandalwood immediately transports them to India. Bags of lentils for dal, sacks of chapati flour and basmati rice, *tavas* (griddle pans), and *thalis* (metal serving plates with bowls) fill the shelves. Outside are colourful displays of fruits and vegetables such as green mangoes and bitter melons for pickling. Customers and shopkeepers haggle over fragrant guavas, bunches of fenugreek, and gleaming green chillies until all are happy with the price.

It is possible to travel the Indian subcontinent while wandering around London. Brick Lane is predominantly Bangladeshi, Southall is Punjabi, and Wembley is Gujarati, while Tooting has a mix of Sri Lankans, Pakistanis, and East Africans. Each neighbourhood has its own shops, restaurants, temples, and mosques. There are also many smaller communities, such as Drummond Street behind Euston Station. Shoppers here buy Indian and Pakistani sweets and snacks for festivals and weddings from the Ambala Sweet Centre on Drummond Street.

SPRING LAMB WITH RAITA, MINT, AND SPRING ONIONS

One of the first signs of spring in London is the arrival of delicate, rosy pink spring lamb from the green hills of Dorset, which appear in butcher shops every March. As the summer progresses, lamb is brought in from further north. Come September, the hill breeds of Scotland and Northumberland are ready for eating. Tender cuts of lamb are preferred by Londoners, who like quickly grilled or roast meats. This recipe is an upmarket version of a kebab, a dish Londoners like to eat when out on the town and in need of a tasty, inexpensive snack. The lamb can be barbecued or char-grilled.

FOR THE MARINADE

1 large onion

Juice of 1 large lemon

Extra virgin olive oil for brushing

Freshly ground pepper

1 kg (2¼ lb) boneless, lean lamb from loin or leg, cut into 2.5 cm (1 inch) cubes

Extra virgin olive oil for brushing

FOR THE RAITA

350 g (12 oz) Greek yoghurt

½ cucumber, peeled and coarsely grated

Fine sea salt and freshly ground pepper

FOR THE SALAD

6 spring or salad onions, white parts only, thinly sliced

4 tablespoons coarsely shredded fresh mint leaves

2 hearts of cos lettuce or Little Gems, coarsely shredded

4 large or 8 small pitta breads

Makes 4 servings

1 To make the marinade, coarsely grate the onion into a fine-mesh sieve set over a large bowl. Press on the onion with the back of a wooden spoon to extract as much juice as possible. Discard the grated onion. Add the lemon juice and olive oil to the onion juice and season with pepper. Add the lamb cubes and turn to coat, then cover with cling film and marinate in the fridge for at least 2 hours or up to 8 hours.

2 To make the raita, put the yoghurt in a serving bowl and whisk in 120 ml (4 fl oz) cold water to form a creamy, thick sauce. Add the cucumber, season to taste with salt and pepper, and stir to combine. Cover and keep in the fridge until needed.

3 If cooking outdoors, prepare a charcoal fire in the barbecue. If using wooden skewers, soak them in water to cover for 30 minutes.

4 To make the salad, in a bowl combine the spring onions, mint, and lettuce. Set aside.

5 Remove the lamb cubes from the marinade and thread on to the skewers. Season with salt and brush with olive oil. Place the kebabs on the barbecue and cook, turning frequently, for 4–6 minutes or until they are well browned; the lamb will be medium-rare. Alternatively, heat a ridged cast-iron grill pan over a moderately high heat. When it is hot, add the kebabs and chargrill, turning frequently, for 4–6 minutes for medium-rare. Remove the lamb cubes from the skewers and add to the salad.

6 Set the pitta breads on the barbecue or grill pan and cook for 1–2 minutes on each side. Split open each pitta bread and fill with the salad and lamb. Spoon in some of the raita and serve at once.

Serve with a pale rosé from Côtes de Provence or a rosato from southern Italy.

PUDDINGS

Rhubarb fool, peach and raspberry trifle, and sticky toffee pudding

reflect the passing seasons in London as surely as the changing weather.

The word dessert used to refer to a course of nuts and dried or sugared fruit offered with Port at the end of a meal, while puddings were sweet dishes served after the main course. Today the terms are used interchangeably, although purists prefer puddings. Whether it is traditional – a boozy trifle, rhubarb fool, fresh apricot crumble, buttery treacle tart, or steamed sticky toffee pudding – or more exotic, such as panna cotta flavoured with rose water, coconut rice pudding with a sweet chilli and pineapple compote, or a deliciously spiced Indian ice cream, no meal is complete without something sweet to finish.

HAZELNUT MERINGUE WITH BLACKBERRIES AND CREAM

A crisp meringue covered in lashings of thickly whipped cream and dewy blackberries makes a luscious dessert. Although they are one of our commonest wild fruits, there is a snobbery about blackberries. This may be because they were regarded as a cheap food for working-class Londoners who used to take their families out blackberrying in the surrounding countryside. They filled every conceivable container with berries from the hedgerows and brought them home to eat with sugar and cream or to make jam. Today's urban cooks buy cultivated blackberries from supermarkets to make pies, crumbles, and mousses.

1 To make the meringue, preheat the oven to 180°C (350°F). Spread the hazelnuts on a baking tray and roast for 15 minutes or until the skins start to wrinkle and flake off. Transfer to a plate. When the nuts are cool enough to handle, pour them on to a tea towel and rub vigorously to remove the skins. Not every speck will come off. Place the hazelnuts in a food processor and pulse 3 or 4 times until finely ground. Set aside.

2 Draw a 20 cm (8 inch) circle on a piece of baking parchment and place on a baking sheet. Put the egg whites in a large, clean bowl. Using a balloon whisk or an electric mixer on medium speed, beat until the whites begin to thicken. Continue to beat, increasing the speed to medium-high if using an electric mixer, just until soft peaks form. Slowly add the caster sugar and continue to beat until medium-firm peaks form. Be careful not to overbeat the whites

or they may start to separate. Sprinkle in the vinegar, salt, and cornflour and fold in with a large metal spoon. Then fold in the ground hazelnuts. Spoon the mixture inside the drawn circle on the prepared baking sheet. Using the metal spoon, neatly shape and flatten into a disc. Place in the oven, reduce the temperature to 150°C (300°F), and bake for 1 hour. Turn off the oven and leave the meringue inside to cool for about 3 hours. The outside will be crisp and the inside will be soft and chewy. Transfer the hazelnut meringue to a serving plate.

3 To make the topping, in a large bowl combine the cream and kirsch, if using. Using a whisk or electric mixer, whip until soft peaks form. Spoon over the meringue and scatter the blackberries on top. Dust with caster sugar. Cut into wedges to serve.

FOR THE MERINGUE

60 g (2 oz) hazelnuts

3 medium egg whites, at room temperature

140 g (5 oz) caster sugar

½ teaspoon white wine vinegar

Pinch of fine sea salt

1 teaspoon cornflour

FOR THE TOPPING

250 ml (8 fl oz) double cream

3 tablespoons kirsch (optional)

350 g (12 oz) blackberries

Caster sugar to dust

Makes 6 servings

SUMMER PUDDING

By July, when markets are piled high with punnets of strawberries, raspberries, and fresh currants, few cooks can resist making a summer pudding. The scent of the warm berries is so enticing that it takes discipline to resist turning out the pudding before it sets. The key to success is to use a good-quality white bread. The bread should have sufficient body to absorb the juice of the cooked fruits and hold its shape, despite being cut into thin slices. If fresh currants are not available, you can replace them with blackberries or blueberries and adjust the sugar to taste.

250 g (9 oz) redcurrants, removed from stalks

250 g (9 oz) blackcurrants, removed from stalks

500 g (1 lb 2 oz) strawberries, hulled and halved

350 g (12 oz) sugar

3 tablespoons raspberry or strawberry eau-de-vie (optional)

250 g (9 oz) raspberries, plus more to garnish

Sunflower oil

8–10 slices good-quality, firm white bread, about 5 mm (¼ inch) thick, crusts removed (see above)

Fresh mint leaves to garnish (optional)

250 ml (8 fl oz) double cream to serve

Makes 6 servings

1 In a non-metallic saucepan, combine the red-and blackcurrants, strawberries, and sugar. Add the eau-de-vie, if using, or 3 tablespoons water. Cover, place over a low heat, and cook, stirring occasionally, for about 5 minutes or until the sugar is dissolved and the fruit releases plenty of juice. Stir in the raspberries and cook, covered, for a further 2 minutes or until the raspberries just begin to release their juices. Leave to cool while you prepare the pudding basin. The fruit will continue to release juice as it cools.

2 Lightly oil a 750 ml (1¼ pint) pudding basin. Cut out a circle of bread that will fit in the bottom of the basin and put it in place. Cut out another circle that will fit inside the top to make a lid, and set aside. Cut the remaining bread slices into wedges or triangles and use them to line the sides of the basin, making sure that there are no gaps between the pieces. The bread should extend above the rim of the basin.

3 Spoon the fruit into the bread-lined basin, packing it gently. It should come to 1 cm (½ inch) below the rim of the basin. Reserve any extra fruit and juice in a covered container in the fridge until ready to serve. Fold in the bread that extends above the rim of the basin over the fruit filling, then cover with the bread lid, pressing down gently. Set a saucer or other small plate on top of the bread lid and weight with a heavy can. Place the basin in a dish to catch any juices, then leave in the fridge for at least 8 hours or up to 2 days.

4 Remove the weight and saucer from the top of the pudding. Run a sharp knife round the inside of the bowl, being careful not to cut into the pudding. Hold an inverted serving plate on top of the basin, then turn over the plate and basin together and shake sharply to remove the pudding from the basin to the plate. Carefully lift off the basin. Pour any reserved juices over the pudding, particularly any bare patches, so that it looks glossy.

5 To serve, garnish the pudding with the reserved fruit or fresh berries and mint leaves, if you like, and serve with a jug of cream.

Serve with a well-chilled sparkling Italian dessert wine such as Freisa or a perfumed white wine such as Malvasia from Piedmont.

PEACH AND RASPBERRY TRIFLE

Each element of a trifle is delicious on its own, but when combined they make an irresistible pudding – even better when the fruit is fresh in season, and the sponge cake and custard are home-made. The earliest recorded trifle recipes date from the sixteenth century, when they were more like spiced and sweetened clotted creams. In the eighteenth century layered trifles were created, using biscuits soaked in sweet wine and a topping of syllabub. The contemporary version here, served in individual glasses, has multiple layers of liqueur-spiked sponge cake, summer fruit, and rich vanilla custard.

1 To make the sponge cake, preheat the oven to 190ºC (375°F). Line a 20 x 30 cm (8 x 12 inch) Swiss roll tin with baking parchment and lightly oil the paper. In a large bowl, using an electric mixer, whisk together the eggs and caster sugar for about 5 minutes or until pale and thick. Using a metal spoon, fold in the flour and salt. Pour into the prepared baking tray and spread evenly. Bake for about 10 minutes or until the cake is golden and springs back when lightly touched with a fingertip.

2 Generously sprinkle caster sugar on a sheet of baking parchment that is slightly larger than the sponge cake. Carefully run a small, thin knife round the inside of the tin to loosen the cake, then turn out on to the sugar-coated paper and lift off the tin. Peel off the lining paper. Leave to cool.

3 Have ready 6 large dessert glasses or bowls. Using a serrated knife, trim the edges of the sponge cake, then cut into 18 pieces that will fit inside the dessert glasses. Wrap the pieces in cling film and set aside.

4 To make the custard, combine the milk, vanilla pod, and granulated sugar in a heavy saucepan. Set over a low heat and stir to dissolve the sugar. Increase the heat to moderate. As soon as small bubbles appear round the edge of the pan, remove from the heat. Leave to infuse for 20 minutes.

5 In a bowl, whisk the egg yolks until smooth. Remove the vanilla pod from the milk and reserve. Whisking constantly, slowly pour the warm milk into the eggs. Return to the saucepan, add the vanilla pod, and set over a low heat. Cook, stirring constantly with a wooden spoon, for 10–20 minutes or until the custard thickens enough to coat the back of the spoon. Do not allow the custard to boil. Strain the custard through a fine-mesh sieve into a bowl. Leave to cool slightly, stirring frequently, then cover with cling film, pressing it on to the surface of the custard to prevent a skin from forming. Chill for at least 1 hour or up to 2 days.

6 To prepare the fruit, combine the liqueur and lemon juice in a bowl. Working over the bowl to catch the juices, cut the peaches into thin slices and let them drop into the bowl. Add the raspberries and stir gently to combine. Set aside to macerate for at least 30 minutes or up to 3 hours.

7 Crumble one cake piece into the bottom of each dessert glass. Spoon 1 tablespoon of the fruit over the cake in each glass and drizzle over a little fruit juice. Drizzle 2 tablespoons of custard over the fruit. Repeat the layering two more times. Cover with cling film and chill for 30 minutes.

8 Just before serving, pour the cream into a large bowl. Using a whisk or electric mixer, whip the cream until soft peaks form. Garnish the top of each trifle with a large dollop of whipped cream, sprinkle with pistachios, if using, and serve.

FOR THE SPONGE CAKE

2 medium eggs

75 g (2½ oz) caster sugar, plus more to sprinkle

60 g (2 oz) plain flour, sifted

Pinch of fine sea salt

FOR THE CUSTARD

400 ml (14 fl oz) whole milk

1 vanilla pod, split in half lengthways

115 g (4 oz) granulated sugar

6 medium egg yolks

FOR THE FRUIT

120 ml (4 fl oz) orange liqueur such as Grand Marnier

1 tablespoon fresh lemon juice

2 ripe peaches, peeled

125 g (4½ oz) raspberries

250 ml (8 fl oz) chilled double cream

2 tablespoons coarsely chopped pistachio nuts (optional)

Makes 6 servings

TREACLE TART

The sticky, sweet character of treacle tart has made it a favourite in gentlemen's clubs and traditional eating establishments, as well as at home, for at least a hundred years. The name may seem misleading, because the filling for treacle tart is made with soft white breadcrumbs mixed with golden syrup. However, although the term treacle is mainly used for the darker syrup that is sometimes called molasses, all of the various sugar syrups produced during sugar refining – including golden syrup, which was introduced in 1883 – can correctly be called treacle. Serve this with pouring cream or vanilla ice cream.

FOR THE PASTRY

300 g (10 oz) plain flour

Pinch of fine sea salt

175 g (6 oz) cold unsalted butter, diced

5–6 tablespoons cold water

FOR THE FILLING

500 ml (16 fl oz) golden syrup or as needed

150 g (5½ oz) fresh white breadcrumbs

Finely grated zest of 2 lemons

Finely grated zest of 1 orange

2 tablespoons fresh lemon juice

1 teaspoon ground ginger

250 ml (8 fl oz) double cream to serve

Makes 8 servings

1 To make the pastry, combine the flour and salt in a large bowl. Rub in the butter until the mixture forms coarse crumbs. Alternatively, place the flour and salt in a food processor, add the butter, and pulse 4 or 5 times until the mixture forms coarse crumbs; transfer to a bowl. Using a fork, stir in enough of the cold water to form a rough dough. Turn the dough out on to a lightly floured work surface and lightly knead just until smooth. Shape the dough into a disc 2 cm (¾ inch) thick, wrap tightly in cling film, and chill for at least 30 minutes or up to overnight.

2 Preheat the oven to 200°C (400°F). On a lightly floured work surface, roll out two-thirds of the dough into a 23 cm (9 inch) round 3 mm (⅛ inch) thick. Drape the dough over the rolling pin and ease into an 18 cm (7 inch) flan tin with a lift-out base, pressing the pastry into place. Use a rolling pin to roll over the edge of the tin to cut off the excess pastry. Prick the pastry case with a fork in several places, then chill for 30 minutes. Add the trimmings to the remaining pastry dough and press together into a disc. Wrap in cling film and keep in the fridge until needed.

3 To make the filling, in a saucepan over a low heat, warm 360 ml (12 fl oz) of the golden syrup until it thins and becomes more liquid. Remove from the heat and stir in the breadcrumbs, lemon and orange zest, lemon juice, and ginger. Leave to soak for about 10 minutes or until the breadcrumbs absorb the syrup.

The mixture should be soft and sticky. If it is stiff and thick, add enough of the remaining golden syrup to achieve the right consistency. Spoon the filling into the pastry case.

4 On a lightly floured work surface, roll out the remaining pastry dough into a rectangle about 18 cm (7 inches) long, 13 cm (5 inches) wide, and 3 mm (⅛ inch) thick. Trim the edges. Cut lengthways into 10 strips about 1 cm (½ inch) wide. Lay 5 of the strips, evenly spaced, over the filling. Lay the remaining 5 strips, evenly spaced, at right angles to the first strips. Trim off the excess dough and crimp to seal to the edge of the pastry case.

5 Bake for 10 minutes, then reduce the oven temperature to 180°C (350°F) and bake for a further 15 minutes or until the pastry is golden. Transfer to a wire rack to cool slightly. Remove the side of the flan tin and transfer the tart to a serving plate. Serve warm or cold, cut into wedges, with cream.

Serve with a nutty, maple-scented dessert wine such as Malmsey Madeira or tawny Port.

STRAWBERRY PAIN PERDU

Pain perdu, French for "lost bread", has been enjoying a revival, no doubt because it is both delicious and easy to make. Its origins date back to the Middle Ages when slices of fine white bread were soaked in egg yolks, fried until crisp in butter, and then liberally sprinkled with sugar. Over the centuries, cinnamon, nutmeg, and other spices have been added, along with alcohol, such as sack, a white wine from Spain, and even cream. More recently, cooks have taken to accompanying pain perdu *with berries or fried bananas.*

1 In a bowl, combine the strawberries and icing sugar. Toss gently and set aside.

2 In a large shallow bowl, whisk together the egg yolks, sherry, caster sugar, and nutmeg. Soak the brioche slices in the egg yolk mixture for 1 minute, turning them at least once.

3 In a large non-stick frying pan over a moderate heat, warm the clarified butter. Remove the brioche slices from the egg yolk mixture and place in the pan. Cook for about 2 minutes or until golden and slightly crisp. Turn and cook until golden and slightly crisp on the other side.

4 Divide the slices among 4 individual plates. Top with the strawberries, garnish with a dollop of crème fraîche, if liked, and serve at once.

Serve with a glass of pink Champagne or a Banyuls from France's Roussillon region.

500 g (1 lb 2 oz) strawberries, hulled and halved

3 tablespoons icing sugar

4 medium egg yolks

4 tablespoons dry sherry

1 tablespoon caster sugar

Pinch of freshly grated nutmeg

4 slices brioche loaf, about 1 cm (½ inch) thick, cut in half diagonally

2 tablespoons clarified unsalted butter (see page 185)

60 g (2 oz) crème fraîche to serve (optional)

Makes 4 servings

English strawberries

By early summer, the London air is sweet with the scent of flowers. The first English strawberries appear in the shops, and Champagne goes on special offer. The summer social season gets started with the Chelsea Flower Show in May and continues with racing at Royal Ascot, tennis at Wimbledon, and rowing at Henley Royal Regatta. Each event calls for dressing up, having fun, and eating delectable food. And no occasion is considered complete without strawberries, preferably accompanied by lashings of cream and a generous sprinkling of sugar. Newspapers even comment on the price of a bowl of strawberries at Wimbledon.

Strawberries have long been sold in London. In medieval times, wild fruit was picked, strung on pieces of straw, and hawked on the streets. By the seventeenth century, new varieties such as the small Hautbois from France and the wild Virginia strawberry from America graced fashionable London tables. Then, in the early nineteenth century, market gardeners like Michael Keens in Isleworth began to create ever bigger hybrids. The French called these large strawberries *les fraises anglaises.*

ROSE WATER PANNA COTTA WITH APPLE COMPOTE

Eating a trembly, creamy panna cotta with seasonal fruit is most Londoners' idea of gustatory bliss. Here, both the panna cotta and the apple compote are subtly scented with rose water, a favourite British flavouring since medieval times. Other floral notes are often added to puddings and syrups – elderflowers in spring, lavender flowers in summer, and orange flower water throughout the year. In the autumn, cooks turn to seasonal apples, pears, and quinces to use in their puddings. Apple varieties that maintain their shape when cooked, such as Braeburn, are best for this compote.

FOR THE PANNA COTTA

750 ml (1¼ pints) double cream

500 ml (16 fl oz) whole milk

3 lemon zest strips

1 tablespoon powdered gelatine

125 g (4½ oz) caster sugar

2 teaspoons rose water

2 tablespoons white dessert wine such as Muscat de Beaumes de Venise

FOR THE APPLE COMPOTE

115 g (4 oz) granulated sugar

Finely grated zest of 1 lemon

1 teaspoon rose water

2 apples, peeled, cored, and diced (see note)

2 tablespoons dried cranberries

2 tablespoons dried blueberries

2 tablespoons dried cherries

2 tablespoons fresh lemon juice

Makes 6 servings

1 To make the panna cotta, combine the cream, milk, and lemon zest in a wide saucepan. Set over a moderately low heat and warm the liquid just until small bubbles appear round the edge of the pan. Reduce the heat to low and simmer gently for about 15 minutes or until reduced by about one-fifth.

2 Meanwhile, place 3 tablespoons water in a large bowl, sprinkle over the gelatine, and allow to soften for about 5 minutes. Pour the hot cream mixture through a fine-mesh sieve into the bowl and stir to dissolve the gelatine. Add the caster sugar and stir until dissolved. Stir in the rose water and wine.

3 Lightly oil six 175 ml (6 fl oz) moulds. Divide the mixture evenly among the moulds. Cover and chill for at least 6 hours or up to overnight.

4 To make the apple compote, combine the sugar, lemon zest, and 120 ml (4 fl oz) water in a saucepan. Set over a moderate heat and cook, stirring occasionally, until the sugar is dissolved. Simmer for about 5 minutes or until the mixture thickens and becomes syrupy. Add the rose water, apples, and dried cranberries, blueberries, and cherries. Reduce the heat to low and simmer for about 5 minutes or just until the apples are tender. Remove from the heat, stir in the lemon juice, and transfer to a serving bowl. Leave to cool to room temperature.

5 To turn out each panna cotta, place the mould in a bowl of hot water for about 10 seconds, then hold an inverted dessert plate over the mould and turn them over together. Shake the mould gently to loosen the panna cotta, and lift off the mould. Spoon the apple compote around and over the top of each panna cotta, dividing it evenly, and serve.

Serve with a sweet, perfumed white wine such as Muscat de Beaumes-de-Venise.

RHUBARB FOOL

Every January, the first pale pink stalks of forced Yorkshire rhubarb appear in London. The plants are forced by transplanting them from the cold Yorkshire ground into warm, dark growing sheds, where they are picked by candlelight until the end of the season in early March. With their fine taste and texture, the slender spears are considered a delicacy. Chefs and home cooks eagerly make rhubarb compote, pies, and crumbles, but rhubarb fool, the stewed fruit folded into whipped cream, is what everyone likes best. Fools are well complemented by small, crisp biscuits, such as sponge fingers or almond tuiles.

1 Trim the ends of the rhubarb and cut into 2.5 cm (1 inch) pieces. Combine the rhubarb, sugar, and 2 tablespoons water in a large saucepan. Set over a moderate heat and cook, stirring occasionally, for about 2 minutes or until the rhubarb begins to release its juice and the sugar is dissolved. Reduce the heat to low, cover, and simmer for a further 5–8 minutes or until the rhubarb is tender and almost completely disintegrated. Remove from the heat and leave to cool to room temperature.

2 In a large bowl, combine the cream and Cointreau, if using. Using a whisk or electric mixer, whip until soft peaks form. Using a metal spoon, fold in the cooked rhubarb and its juice so that pink ripples are created through the cream.

3 Divide the rhubarb fool among dessert glasses and chill for at least 1 hour before serving.

Serve with a chilled Italian sparkling wine such as Prosecco or Freisa.

500 g (1 lb 2 oz) rhubarb

225 g (8 oz) sugar

250 ml (8 fl oz) very cold double cream

3 tablespoons Cointreau (optional)

Makes 6 servings

STICKY TOFFEE PUDDING

Steamed puddings became fashionable in the seventeenth century with the invention of the pudding cloth, a piece of fabric that was tied around the pudding mixture to make a ball, so it could be boiled in a pot. In the nineteenth century, wooden and china pudding basins replaced the cloth. Whether sweet or savoury, the early puddings often contained spices and "plums", which referred to any variety of dried fruit. Initially, they were moistened with eggs, suet, or bone marrow, but by the nineteenth century, raising agents were used to create light puddings, such as this one studded with dates.

FOR THE PUDDING

250 g (9 oz) pitted Medjool dates, finely chopped

120 ml (4 fl oz) very hot tea such as Earl Grey

190 g (6½ oz) plain flour

1 teaspoon baking powder

85 g (3 oz) unsalted butter, at room temperature

175 g (6 oz) light soft brown sugar

½ teaspoon pure vanilla extract

2 medium eggs

1 tablespoon brandy

FOR THE TOFFEE SAUCE

200 g (7 oz) light soft brown sugar

115 g (4 oz) unsalted butter

90 ml (3 fl oz) double cream

2 tablespoons brandy

Pinch of fine sea salt

Makes 6 servings

1 To make the pudding, combine the chopped dates and hot tea in a small bowl and soak for 30 minutes.

2 Generously butter six 175 ml (6 fl oz) dariole moulds or a 1 litre (2 pint) pudding basin. Cut out circles of baking parchment to fit the top and bottom of the moulds or basin. Place the bottom circle(s) in place. Select a wide, deep pan or saucepan that will hold the moulds or basin and half fill with water. Bring to the boil.

3 Meanwhile, sift the flour and baking powder into a bowl and set aside. In another bowl, using an electric mixer on medium-high speed, beat the butter and brown sugar for about 2 minutes or until fluffy. Beat in the vanilla extract. Add the eggs and brandy and beat until pale and fluffy. Add the flour mixture and beat on low speed just until incorporated. Using a wooden spoon, stir in the dates and any soaking liquid.

4 Spoon the mixture into the moulds or basin, smooth the top, and cover with the remaining circle(s) of parchment. Then cover the moulds or basin with foil, pleated in the centre to allow the pudding to rise as it cooks, tying on the foil with string under the rim to form a tight seal.

5 Carefully lower the moulds or basin into the pan of boiling water; the water should come no higher than the string tied round the moulds or basin. Cover the pan and steam until a knife inserted in the centre of a pudding comes out clean, about 45 minutes for the individual puddings or 2 hours for the large pudding. Check the water level occasionally and top up if necessary. Lift the moulds or basin from the saucepan and allow to stand for 10 minutes.

6 While the pudding is resting, make the sauce. In a small saucepan, combine the brown sugar, butter, cream, brandy, and salt. Set over a low heat and cook, stirring occasionally, until the sugar is dissolved and the butter is melted. Bring to the boil and cook, stirring frequently, for about 4 minutes or until the sauce has thickened and darkened.

7 Remove the foil and top parchment circle from each pudding. Run a sharp knife around the edge of the pudding, then turn out on to a serving plate. Peel off the bottom circle of paper. Pour some of the warm sauce over the puddings and serve with the remaining sauce.

Serve with a rich, complex sweet dessert wine such as Madeira or tawny Port.

OATCAKES WITH CHEESE AND CELERY

Londoners are spoiled by the array of superb cheeses they can buy in specialist shops such as Neal's Yard Dairy or La Fromagerie, and they like to serve cheese as a separate course at dinner parties – before, after, or instead of the pudding. The preferred accompaniments are a selection of savoury biscuits, such as oatcakes, water biscuits, or Bath Olivers, and crisp celery. Freshly baked oatcakes are particularly delicious partners for a lemony fresh goat's cheese, a blue cheese such as Stilton, and a crumbly Wensleydale or the Devonshire sheep's milk cheese Beenleigh Blue.

1 Preheat the oven to 190ºC (375°F). Line 2 baking sheets with baking parchment.

2 In a bowl, stir together the oatmeal, flour, bicarbonate of soda, and salt. Using a wooden spoon, stir in the melted butter and warm water. Using your hands, mix to form a stiff, slightly sticky dough. The dough should be pliant enough to roll; if necessary, sprinkle on a little more warm water and mix in with your hands.

3 Turn the dough out on to a lightly floured work surface. Dust a rolling pin with flour and roll out the dough into a round 3 mm (⅛ inch) thick. If the dough keeps breaking up, return it to the bowl, add a few more drops of warm water, and mix again with your hands. With a floured 5.5 cm (2¼ inch) round cutter and, using a quick, sharp motion, cut out oatcakes as close together as possible. Gather the scraps of dough, roll out, and cut additional rounds. Place them 2.5 cm (1 inch) apart on the prepared baking sheets. Bake for about 12 minutes or until the oatcakes are lightly coloured and crisp. Transfer to a wire rack to cool. The oatcakes can be stored in an airtight tin for up to a month.

4 About 15 minutes before serving, arrange the cheeses on a cheeseboard or a platter and allow to come to room temperature. Place the oatcakes in a basket and the celery in a glass, and allow guests to help themselves.

115 g (4 oz) medium oatmeal

1 tablespoon plain flour

½ teaspoon bicarbonate of soda

¼ teaspoon fine sea salt

1½ tablespoons melted unsalted butter

120 ml (4 fl oz) warm water, or as needed

A selection of cheeses, such as a fresh goat's cheese, a blue-veined cheese, and a mature cow's or sheep's milk cheese (see above)

1 bunch celery, separated into sticks and trimmed

Makes 4–6 servings

COCONUT RICE PUDDING WITH PINEAPPLE IN CHILLI SYRUP

The multicultural character of London has led to an astounding fusion of cuisines. In the kitchen of a large restaurant, Caribbean, Indian, Moroccan, Australian, New Zealand, Thai, African, and British chefs might be working alongside those from different European nationalities. As a result, flavouring an Anglo-Indian rice pudding with Caribbean rum and coconut and serving it with an Australian-influenced spiced pineapple compote seems natural. The combination is utterly delicious and curiously British.

1 To make the rice pudding, preheat the oven to 150°C (300°F). Generously butter a 1 litre (2 pint) baking dish.

2 In a bowl, stir together the rice, coconut, brown sugar, cinnamon, and salt. Transfer to the baking dish. In the same bowl, stir together the milk, cream, and rum. Pour over the rice. Bake for 30 minutes. Remove from the oven and stir. Reduce the oven temperature to 135°C (275°F) and bake, stirring occasionally, for a further 1 hour or until the rice is meltingly tender and most of the liquid has been absorbed.

3 Meanwhile, prepare the pineapple compote. Combine the granulated sugar, chilli, star anise, cloves, and 250 ml (8 fl oz) water in a small saucepan. Bring to the boil, stirring occasionally, until the sugar is dissolved, then continue to cook for about 10 minutes or until a thick syrup forms.

4 While the syrup is cooking, cut the green crown off the pineapple, then cut a thin slice from the base. Stand the pineapple upright and, using a large, sharp knife, cut the peel away in vertical strips. Lay the pineapple on its side and align the blade with the diagonal rows of brown "eyes". Working in a spiral, cut at an angle on each side of the eyes to remove them. Cut the pineapple lengthways into quarters. Remove the tough core from each quarter, then thinly slice crossways. Place in a shallow bowl. Pour the syrup over the pineapple and cool to room temperature. Serve the pudding warm, at room temperature, or cold with the pineapple compote.

FOR THE RICE PUDDING

60 g (2 oz) Arborio rice

3 tablespoons desiccated coconut

175 g (6 oz) light soft brown sugar

½ teaspoon ground cinnamon

Pinch of fine sea salt

550 ml (18 fl oz) whole milk

150 ml (5 fl oz) double cream

3 tablespoons dark rum

FOR THE PINEAPPLE COMPOTE

115 g (4 oz) granulated sugar

¼ fresh red or green chilli, seeded and finely sliced

1 star anise

2 cloves

1 medium pineapple

Makes 4 servings

Mangoes

South American mangoes are sold in London throughout the year, but the true mango season begins in May. This is when the first crates of Alphonso mangoes from India and Pakistan arrive at the Great Western Market, just outside Heathrow Airport. The matte, yellow skin of this plump variety hides aromatic, non-fibrous, yellow flesh that is utterly delicious. They are packed six or twelve to a box, wrapped in crumpled paper with a few glittering strands of tinsel.

Boxes of Alphonso mangoes are stacked high in every Indian, Pakistani, and Middle Eastern food shop in the city. Canny shoppers carefully inspect the contents of each box. Ripe mangoes release a fragrance near their stalk end and yield slightly to gentle pressure. Bruised, wrinkled, or very soft specimens are surreptitiously swapped for better fruits from other boxes before the shopper tries, often unsuccessfully, to bargain over the price. Once home, a whole box of mangoes can frequently be eaten in a few days. The season continues through June as other Indian varieties come on the market, such as honeyed Banganpali mangoes and sweet Kesar mangoes.

PEAR SOUFFLÉ

Dipping a spoon into an ethereal pear soufflé redolent of Poire William, the aromatic pear brandy, is sure to create a hush around the dinner table. In the 1950s and 1960s, every London debutante aspired to make a soufflé in a bid to woo a husband. The dessert fell out of favour but was reintroduced by Albert and Michel Roux, the influential cutting-edge chefs who opened the Michelin-starred Le Gavroche in London in 1967, followed by Michel Roux's Waterside Inn in Berkshire. They are credited with creating the fashion for delicate fruit soufflés with a layer of macerated fruit in the centre.

4 large ripe pears such as Comice, about 750 g (1 lb 10 oz) total weight

115 g (4 oz) granulated sugar, plus more to coat

Juice of 1 lemon

2 tablespoons arrowroot

4 tablespoons Poire William

1 tablespoon melted unsalted butter

4 medium egg whites

Makes 8 servings

1 Peel and core 3 of the pears and coarsely dice. Combine the diced pears, sugar, and half of the lemon juice in a small saucepan. Set over a moderately low heat and cook for about 15 minutes or until the pears are meltingly soft. Transfer to a food processor and purée until smooth. Return to the pan.

2 Put the arrowroot in a small bowl and slowly stir in 3 tablespoons of the Poire William until smooth. Using a wooden spoon, stir into the puréed pears. Bring to the boil and cook, stirring constantly, until thickened. Remove from the heat and allow to cool for 1 hour.

3 Peel and core the remaining pear, then finely dice. Place in a bowl and stir in the remaining Poire William and lemon juice. Set aside to macerate for at least 20 minutes or up to 40 minutes.

4 Place a heavy baking sheet in the oven and preheat to 220ºC (425°F). Brush 8 large ramekins with the melted butter and evenly coat with granulated sugar, shaking out the excess.

5 Drain the diced pears, reserving the liquid. Stir the liquid into the puréed pears. Put the egg whites in a large, clean bowl. Using a balloon whisk or an electric mixer on medium speed, beat until the whites begin to thicken. Continue to beat, increasing the speed to medium-high if using an electric mixer, just until soft, floppy peaks form. Using a metal spoon, fold one-third of the egg whites into the puréed pears to lighten. Gently fold in the remaining egg whites just until no white streaks remain.

6 Spoon the soufflé mixture into the prepared ramekins to half fill them. Sprinkle with the diced pears, dividing evenly. Top with the remaining soufflé mixture. Tap each ramekin on a work surface to settle the contents. Place on the hot baking sheet, reduce the oven temperature to 180ºC (350°F), and bake for about 10 minutes or until well risen but still slightly wobbly. Serve immediately.

Serve with a late-harvest Chenin Blanc such as a Savennières or Montlouis.

FERMENTED BLACK BEANS Sometimes called salted or preserved black beans, these pungent beans are soya beans that have been dried, salted, and allowed to ferment until they turn black. The beans should be rinsed gently in a fine-mesh sieve to remove excess salt before using in a recipe. They are sold in plastic bags and will keep for a year if stored in a cool, dry place.

GARAM MASALA This blend of whole or ground spices from northern India (*garam masala* means simply "spice blend") generally includes black pepper, cardamom, cinnamon, cloves, coriander, cumin, dried chillies, fennel, mace, and nutmeg. For optimal freshness, store garam masala in a cool, dry place for no longer than 6 months.

GELATINE Made from animal protein, gelatine is a colourless, flavourless thickener available as fine granules/powder and in sheets. To use powdered gelatine, soften it, without stirring, in cold liquid, then stir thoroughly into the liquid to be jellied and heat it gently without allowing it to boil. When cooled, the mixture will set into a firm mass.

GLACÉ CHERRIES These candied cherries are used in mincemeat and as a decoration. Store in an airtight container in a cool, dry place.

GOLDEN SYRUP A clear, golden liquid sweetener made from refined cane sugar, this is used both as a topping and spread and as an ingredient in cake, biscuit, and other sweet recipes.

GREEK YOGHURT Made from cow's or sheep's milk, Greek yoghurt is thicker and less sour than other types of yoghurts. If Greek yoghurt is unavailable, you can make your own version: place plain whole milk yoghurt in a colander lined with muslin set over a bowl and leave to drain overnight in the fridge.

GREEN CARDAMOM PODS Belonging to the ginger family, the cardamom plant bears pods containing seeds that have a spicy, aromatic flavour. Green cardamom has the most delicate flavour and is the most popular type. When ground, the seeds give off a camphorlike aroma, although the taste is sweet and mild. For the freshest results, buy whole pods and remove and grind the seeds as needed.

HADDOCK, SMOKED AND FRESH This mild-flavoured and lean white-fleshed fish can be cooked by most methods, except on the barbecue, where it might fall apart. Cod, with its similar taste and texture, can be used interchangeably with haddock. When smoked – as a whole split fish or in fillets – pale, naturally cured haddock is preferable to the bright yellow, artificially coloured variety.

HORSERADISH Native to Europe and Asia, this gnarled root has a pungent flavour that contributes a spicy bite to sauces and side dishes and pairs well with roast beef. If fresh horseradish is not available, you can substitute bottled horseradish that has been grated and mixed with vinegar.

LEMONGRASS This long, slender, fibrous, lemon-scented grass native to Southeast Asia is a staple flavouring in many cuisines of the region. The bulbous base is either pounded or thinly sliced to release its fragrance; the coarse upper portion is discarded. If fresh lemongrass is unavailable, you can substitute 1 tablespoon slivered lemon balm or chopped lemon zest. Lemongrass will keep for up to 2 weeks in the fridge.

MANDARIN PEEL, DRIED The dried peel of mandarin oranges is used as a flavouring in many Chinese dishes. It is sold whole or ground in Chinese food shops. Dried tangerine peel or orange peel can be substituted.

MEDJOOL DATES Classified as soft dates, Medjool dates have a high moisture content and soft texture. Although their dry, sticky exterior suggests that they are dried fruits, most dates are sold fresh. They should be tightly wrapped in plastic and will keep in the fridge for up to 3 weeks.

OYSTER SAUCE A concentrated dark brown sauce made from dried oysters, salt, water, cornflour, and caramel. The slightly sweet, smoky-flavoured sauce originated in southern China. The least expensive sauces lack a rich oyster flavour. Once the bottle is opened, store oyster sauce in the fridge.

PHEASANT Farmed birds have a less strong gamey flavour than their wild cousins, and females (hens) tend to be plumper and more tender than males (cocks). You can buy pheasants whole, boned, or as boneless breasts in supermarkets and butchers.

POIRE WILLIAM Fruit brandies, or eaux-de-vie, are distilled liquors produced from a variety of fruits. The most common brandy is made with grapes.

Poire William is derived from pears, framboise from raspberries, kirsch from cherries, and calvados from apples. These fruit brandies are not sweet but are imbued with the intense fragrance and flavour of the fruit from which they are made. It often takes as much as 9 kg (18 lb) of fruit to produce a small bottle of eau-de-vie.

POMEGRANATE MOLASSES This thick syrup is made from reduced pomegranate juice. The final product is not strictly molasses, but the term refers to the liquid's thick, syrupy texture. Long a staple in Middle Eastern cooking, pomegranate molasses is being increasingly used in London in sauces, soups, and salad dressings. It is available in most Middle Eastern food shops.

PROSCIUTTO Italian ham that is seasoned, salt-cured, and air-dried. Its distinctive fragrance and subtle flavour make prosciutto one of the world's favourite hams. Prosciutto from Parma, which is aged from 10 months to 2 years, is considered to be among the best.

QUAIL'S EGGS Although much smaller than hen's eggs, quail's eggs have a similar flavour and texture. With shells speckled in colour from dark brown to blue and white, they are attractive to serve hard-boiled in the shell as an hors d'oeuvre, a garnish, or an accompaniment for salads. Five quail's eggs are equivalent to one chicken's egg.

QUINCE A relative of the rose, the quince resembles a misshapen yellow apple. The hard, dry flesh has an intensely astringent flavour when raw. Once cooked, however, the flesh becomes a deep rose pink and gains a heady fragrance. Quinces are available October to December at speciality green-grocers and many supermarkets. Store unripe fruits at cool room temperature; ripe quinces can be kept in a plastic bag in the fridge for up to 2 weeks.

RHUBARB The long, celerylike stalks of rhubarb are very sour when raw but gain a soft texture and appealing tartness when cooked with sugar to use in pies and tarts, fools, and other puddings, as well as jams, preserves, chutneys, and sauces for savoury dishes. The stalks range in colour from bright red to pink streaked with pale green. The leaves contain oxalic acid, a potentially toxic substance, and should be discarded. Forced (indoor) rhubarb is available at the beginning of the year; outdoor-grown rhubarb is in season from spring to early summer.

ROCKET This peppery green has deeply notched leaves about 5 cm (2 inches) long; the leaves of wild rocket are smaller and more ragged. Rocket is sold in bunches or as loose leaves in packets.

ROSE WATER Derived from a distillation of rose petals, rose water has an intensely aromatic flavour and fragrance. It has been used for centuries as a flavouring in Middle Eastern, Indian, and English cuisines. Rose water is available in Middle Eastern food shops and delicatessens.

SCALLOPS The white flesh of these popular bivalves has a smooth texture and an appealing sweetness. If the scallops are still in their shell, the bright orange roe, or "coral", will still be attached; the coral is a great delicacy. Scallops sold loose out of their shells will usually be without the corals. Buy scallops the day you plan to serve them and keep in the fridge until ready to use.

SORREL A long, narrow leaf appreciated for its highly acidic, tart, almost lemony flavour. The delicate leaves have the unusual ability to melt into a purée when exposed to heat and are a popular source of flavouring in sauces, soups, and stuffings. Very young leaves are used raw in salads.

SOY SAUCE, NATURALLY BREWED A ubiquitous oriental seasoning, made from fermented soya bean meal and wheat. Naturally brewed soy sauce has a full-bodied taste and is superior to the synthetic versions containing sweeteners and colouring agents.

STAR ANISE The star-shaped pod, or fruit, borne by a small evergreen tree of the magnolia family. The seed-bearing pods are picked when they are unripe and then are dried. Their flavour and aroma are sweet, strong, and liquorice-like. Despite the name, star anise is not related to anise.

TAHINI This paste made from ground sesame seeds has a rich, creamy flavour and a concentrated sesame taste. Tahini is an essential ingredient in houmous, baba ghanoush, and other Middle Eastern dishes. Be sure to stir before using, as the oil often separates out from the paste.

THAI FISH SAUCE A thin, clear liquid made from salted and fermented fish and ranging in colour from amber to dark brown. It has a pungent aroma and a strong, salty flavour. Southeast Asians use fish sauce in the same way that Westerners use salt, both as a seasoning when cooking and at the table. Bottles of Thai fish sauce are often labelled *nam pla*. Fish sauce from Vietnam is called *nuoc cham*.

TOASTED SESAME OIL Extracted from toasted sesame seeds, sesame oil is a fragrant, deep amber oil used primarily in Japan, Korea, and China as a flavouring rather than a cooking oil.

TOMATOES Round, plum, and cherry are the three basic types of tomatoes. Medium or large round tomatoes are excellent for slicing, while egg-shaped plum tomatoes have more pulp and less juice, which makes them ideal for sauces. Small cherry tomatoes are available in a variety of colours.

SKINNING AND SEEDING TOMATOES: Cut an X in the skin at the blossom end of each tomato. Immerse in a pan of boiling water until the skin begins to curl away from the X. Transfer to a bowl of iced water to cool briefly, then peel away the skin. To remove the seeds, cut the tomato in half crossways and squeeze each half gently to dislodge the seeds.

TURMERIC A member of the ginger family, this spice is valued for its earthy flavour and intense yellow-orange colour. Widely grown and processed in India, turmeric is the main ingredient in commercial curry powder. It is most often used in its dried, ground form. Fresh turmeric root, which resembles fresh ginger, is essential in Southeast Asian cooking.

INGREDIENT SOURCES

A GOLD
Cakes, biscuits, tea, fudge, sugar mice, ginger brack, British vinegars, chutneys, pickles, and preserves
020 7247 2487
www.agold.co.uk

BERRY BROS & RUDD LTD
An enormous range of wines, Ports, and spirits
020 7739 9600
www.bbr.com

FORTNUM & MASON
Specialist teas, preserves, biscuits, chocolates, marmalades, rose petal jams, and honey
020 7734 8040
www.fortnumandmason.com

H FORMAN & SON
Smoked fish, including wild salmon, hot smoked salmon, royal fillets, and smoked haddock
020 8221 3900
www.formanandfield.com

NEAL'S YARD DAIRY
British cheeses such as Stilton, Cheddar, Cheshire, and Lancashire
020 7645 3555
ww.nealsyarddairy.co.uk

SHIPTON MILL
Stone-ground flours including organic oatmeal for oatcakes, organic white flour, and coarse brown bread flour
01666 505050
enquiries@shipton-mill.com

INDEX

A

Afternoon tea, 32–35, 69–80

Almonds
    and apricot crumble, 176
    lemon and lavender drizzle cake, 79

Apples
    compote, rose water panna cotta with, 168
    mince pies, 80

Apricot and almond crumble, 176

Armagnac
    about, 185
    spiced brandy prunes, 183

Asparagus, 109

Assam tea, 185

Avocado, spicy crab, and watercress
    salad, 106

B

Bacon
    and egg butties, 139
    seared scallops with tagliatelle, broad beans,
      and, 144

Bakeries, 62–65

Bangers and mash with red onion
    and wine gravy, 128

Bars, 58. *See also* Pubs

Beans. *See* Black beans; Broad beans; Chickpeas

Beef
    Cornish pasties, 65
    roast, and Yorkshire pudding, 140
    steak, mushroom, and ale pie, 136

Beer, 50, 52

Black beans, fermented, 186

Blackberries, hazelnut meringue
    with cream and, 159

Blini with smoked salmon and crème fraîche, 87

The Bramble, 60

Bread. *See also* Bakeries; Sandwiches
    brioche, 185
    strawberry *pain perdu,* 167
    summer pudding, 160
    treacle tart, 164

Breweries, 52

Brioche. *See* Bread

Broad beans
    seared scallops with tagliatelle, bacon, and,
      144
    skinning, 186

Buckwheat flour, 185

Bulgur wheat
    about, 185
    Mediterranean mezze, 99

Buns, hot cross, 34, 72

Butter, clarified, 185

Butties, bacon and egg, 139

C

Cafés, 139

Caipirinha, 61

Cakes
    chocolate fairy, 71
    coffee and walnut, 35
    jolly rich fruit, 35
    lemon and lavender drizzle, 79
    Victoria sponge, 34

Cardamom pods, green, 186

Celery, oatcakes with cheese and, 175

Celeriac
    about, 185
    vegetable crisps, 91

Chamomile tea, 40

Champagne cocktail, 61

Cheese
    feta, chicory, pear, and walnut
      salad, 110
    and ham scones, 76
    -mongers, 46
    oatcakes with celery and, 175
    omelette Arnold Bennett, 143
    quince, 118
    Stilton and leek tart, 95
    varieties of, 46, 48–49

Cherries, glacé
    about, 186
    mince pies, 80

Chicken tikka masala, 151

Chicory
    about, 185
    salad, pear, feta, walnut and, 110

Chickpeas
    Mediterranean mezze, 99
    salad, tomato, chorizo, and, 105

Chillies, 185

Chocolate
    fairy cakes, 71
    shops, 71

Chorizo. *See* Sausage

Citrus peel, candied, 185

Cocktails, 58, 60–61

Coconut
    raspberry slices, 34
    rice pudding with pineapple, 179

Cod
    about, 56
    fish and chips, 127
    fish pie, 147

Coffee
    bars, 139
    -houses, 79
    tea vs., 40, 79
    vodka espresso, 61
    and walnut cake, 35

Cointreau, 185

Collins, flavoured, 61

Crab
    brown, 57
    salad, avocado, watercress, and spicy, 106

Crème fraîche, 185

Crisps, vegetable, 91

Crumble, apricot and almond, 176

Crumpets, 35

Cucumbers
    about, 113
    raita, 152
    soup, chilled, 113

Cuisine, London
    contemporary, 15–16
    foreign influences on, 11, 12–13, 117, 151
    history of, 11–13

Currants
    about, 185
    hot cross buns, 34, 72
    mince pies, 80
    summer pudding, 160

ACKNOWLEDGMENTS

Sybil Kapoor would like to thank Raj Kapoor, Lorna Wing, Louise Mackaness, Jean-Blaise Hall, Rosemary Scoular, Sophie Laurimore, Caroline Stacey, Jonathan Downey, Susan Low, Gerhard Jenne, Vineet Bhatia, Nino Sassu, Randolph Hodgson, Patricia Michelson, Nick Strangeway, Harriet Docker, Lindsay Stewart, and Peter Haydon for all their help, as well as the many other Londoners who gladly supplied information whenever it was needed. She would also like to thank the team at Weldon Owen, including Hannah Rahill, Kim Goodfriend, and Nicky Collings.

Weldon Owen and the photography team would like to give an especially big thank-you to the fabulous employees and owners of Assaggi, Bramah Museum of Tea and Coffee, Cecconi's, Club Gascon, Fergus Henderson and the employees of St John Bar and Restaurant and St John Bread & Wine (and for the best Eccles cake we've ever tasted); John Duffell and Steve Duffell of Cranleigh Fishmongers; Ken and Maria (Mum) Collings; Le Truc Vert; No. 6 George Street Restaurant and Shop; E&O (especially our favorite bartender!); Rasoi Vineet Bhatia; Sandra Hanauer for her beautiful cakes and other teatime treats; The Jerusalem Tavern; The Westbourne Pub; West Cornwall Pasty Co., and the local farmers' markets, seafood and meat markets, street markets, and covered markets of London. They also wish to extend their gratitude to the owners and workers of the restaurants, bakeries, shops, and other culinary businesses in London who participated in this project: & Clarke's, A. Gold, Baker & Spice, Berry Bros. & Rudd, Books for Cooks, Café des Amis Wine Bar, Camisa & Son, Chalmers & Gray, C. Lidgate Butcher and Charcutier, Charbonnel et Walker, Churchill Arms, Coach & Horses, Costas Fish Restaurants, Fifteen, Floridita, Fortnum & Mason, Fresh & Wild, Gerry's Wine and Spirits, Golborne Fisheries, Gordon Ramsay at Claridge's, Hakkasan, Harrod's, Konditor & Cook, L'Artisan du Chocolat, La Fromagerie, Lamb & Flag, Le Gavroche, Lina Stores, London Chocolate Society, Masters Super Fish, Match Bar, Moro, Neal's Yard Dairy, Patisserie Valerie, Paxton and Whitfield, Rococo Chocolates, Sketch, Speck, Talad Thai, Tamarind, The Eagle Pub, The Fish Shop, The George Inn, The Ginger Pig, The Oak, The Palm Court at The Ritz, The Pie Man, The River Café, The Townhouse, Vama, Yauatcha, Zafferano, and Zuma. For the beautiful props, a special thank-you to Summerill & Bishop, including owners Bernadette, June, and Aurolie, and to The Conran Shop. The team would also like to thank Garibaldi's and Pacific Coast Brewing Co. in Oakland, California, and Elite Café in San Francisco, California.

Weldon Owen also wishes to thank the following individuals for their kind assistance: Desne Ahlers, Ken DellaPenta, Leslie Evans, Judith Dunham, Carolyn R. Keating, Denise Santoro Lincoln, Lorna Wing, and Sharron Wood

PHOTO CREDITS
Jean-Blaise Hall, all photography, except for the following:
Francesca Yorke: Front cover (bottom), Pages 52 (bottom), 92, 116, 128, 133, 136, 139, 147, 149, 160, 162, 176
Martin Brigdale: Pages 72, 121, 134, 143, 152, 181, 183

PHOTOGRAPHY LOCATIONS

The following London locations have been given references for the map on pages 28–29.

PAGE	LOCATION (MAP COORDINATES)
2	C. Lidgate Butcher (C5)
4	Knightsbridge (E5–F5)
8	Burlington Gardens (H4)
12	(right) Harrod's (F6)
14	The River Café
15	(upper) Zuma (F5)
16	(left) Hakkasan (H3)
17	(upper) Fifteen (K2)
20	Portobello Road Market (C4)
27	(left) L'Artisan du Chocolate (F7); (right) Yauatcha (H4)
30	La Fromagerie (B1)
38	Bramah Museum of Tea and Coffee (K5)
43	(bottom right) A. Gold (L3)
45	Camisa & Son (H4)
46	Paxton and Whitfield (H4)
47	(upper) Neal's Yard Dairy (H4)
51	(upper) Barrett Street (G4)
55	(upper) Chalmers & Gray (C5); (center) Golborne Fisheries (C3);(lower right) The Fish Shop (C5)
58	Hakkasan (H3)
62	Baker & Spice (G6)
63	(upper) & Clarke's (C5)
64	West Cornwall Pasty Co.
66	The Palm Court at The Ritz (G5)
71	Charbonnel et Walker (G5)
73	Westminster Abbey (H5)
79	Books for Cooks (C4)
81	Regent Street (G4)
82	Zafferano (F5)
84	(upper right) Covent Garden Market (I4); (lower left) Tower Bridge (L5); (lower right) Brick Lane (L3)
90	Floridita (H4)
93	Talad Thai restaurant
97	Tamarind (G5)
98	Aldar on Edgware Road (F4)
100	Portobello Road Market (C4)
110	Harrod's (F6)
112	Trafalgar Square (H4)
120	Portobello Road Market (C4)
122	Zuma (F5)
130	Berry Bros. & Rudd (H5)
137	C. Lidgate Butcher (C5)
140	Churchill Arms (D5)
146	Golborne Fisheries (C3)
153	Barrett Street (G4)
154	Sketch (G4)
161	Hyde Park (E4–F5)
170	St. Pancras Station (G3)
173	Baker & Spice (G6)
177	Books for Cooks (C4)
180	Le Gavroche (F4)